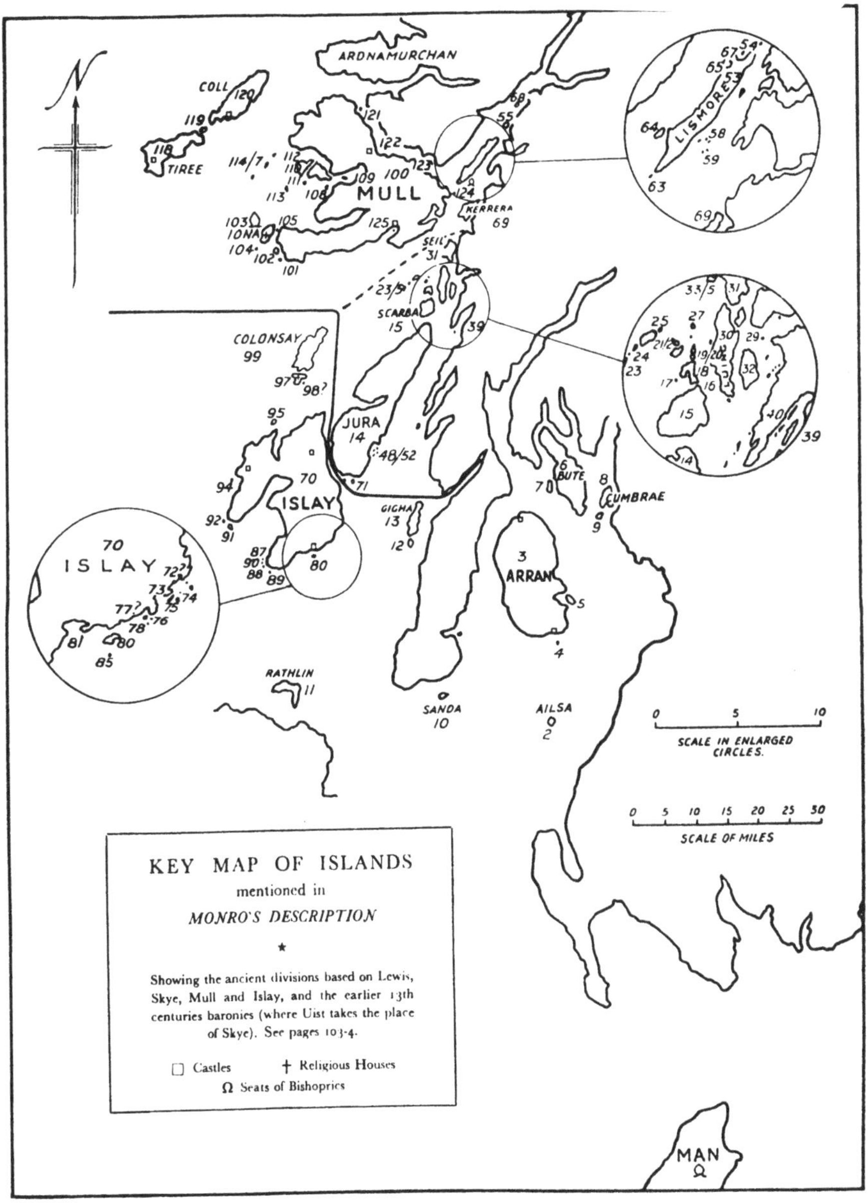

KEY MAP OF ISLANDS

mentioned in

MONRO'S DESCRIPTION

★

Showing the ancient divisions based on Lewis, Skye, Mull and Islay, and the earlier 13th centuries baronies (where Uist takes the place of Skye). See pages 103-4.

□ Castles ✝ Religious Houses

Ω Seats of Bishoprics

SCALE IN ENLARGED CIRCLES.

SCALE OF MILES

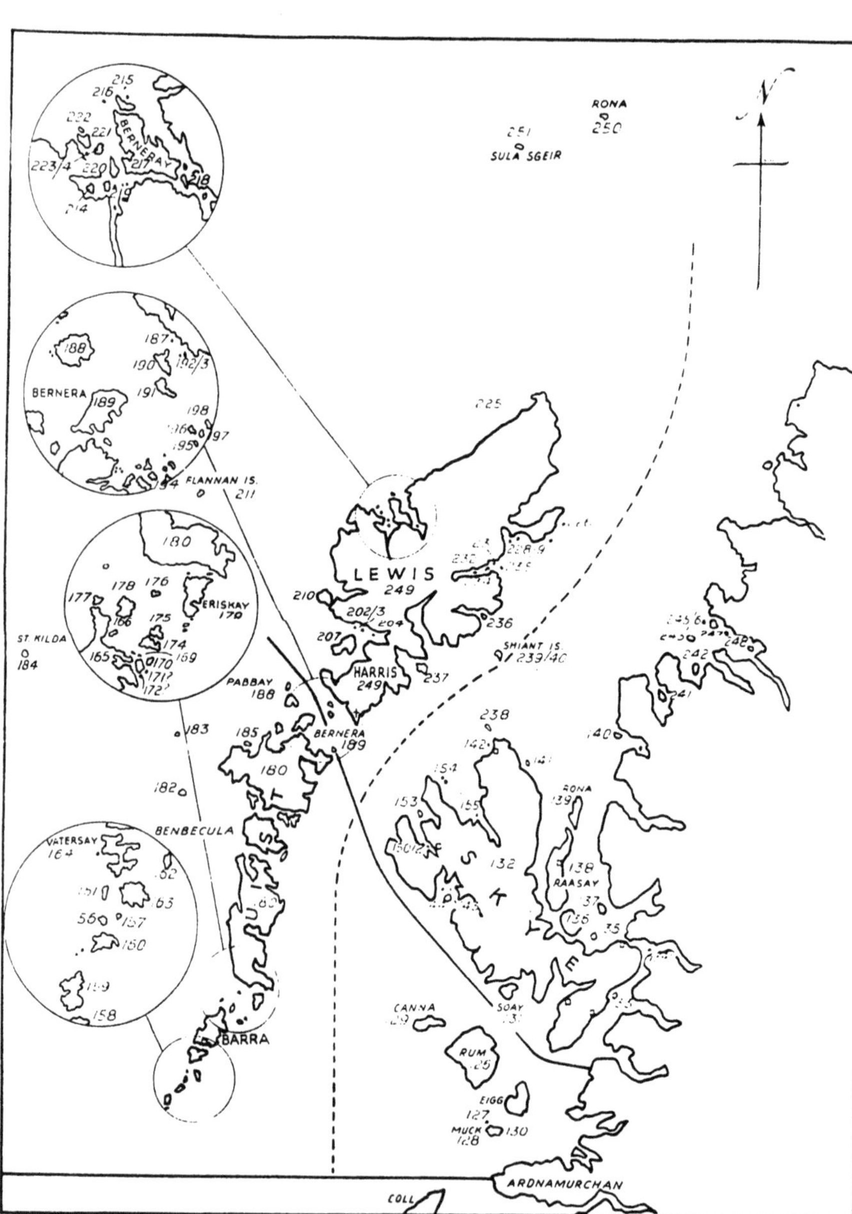
RONA
250
251
SULA SGEIR
BERNERAY
BERNERA
FLANNAN IS.
211
ERISKAY
ST. KILDA
184
LEWIS
249
HARRIS
249
SHIANT IS.
239/40
PABBAY
188
BERNERA
189
BENBECULA
VATERSAY
164
BARRA
SKYE
RONA
139
RAASAY
CANNA
SOAY
RUM
EIGG
127
MUCK
128
130
COLL
ARDNAMURCHAN

MONRO'S WESTERN ISLES OF SCOTLAND AND GENEALOGIES OF THE CLANS

1549

EDITED FROM A HITHERTO UNPUBLISHED MS.
WITH INTRODUCTION AND NOTES BY

R. W. MUNRO

CLEARFIELD COMPANY

First Published 1961

Reprinted for
Clearfield Company, Inc. by
Genealogical Publishing Co., Inc.
Baltimore, Maryland
1993

International Standard Book Number 0-8063-5076-8

FOREWORD

SOME years ago, while examining the manuscripts of Donald Monro's 'Description of the Western Isles of Scotland' in the National Library, I happened to light upon a better and fuller version than those already published. It had apparently been seen by others, but never printed; it shows that the author has suffered more than has been realised from mutilation and inaccurate copying; and it fills many important gaps left in former texts, as well as correcting some of their mistakes.

Monro's is the earliest known description of the Western Isles from personal observation. It formed the basis of George Buchanan's account of them, at the beginning of his Latin *History of Scotland*. A comparison of the two, however, shows that there are considerable omissions in previous editions of Monro's work; these have now been made good, with the recovery of his account of more than forty islands, and of the 'Council of the Isles' at Finlaggan which had hitherto been missing.

In adding a new, and basically different, edition to those which already bear Donald Monro's name (and earned him fame in spite of their shortcomings), I have tried to give the reader whatever might be useful in appreciating the work and its author. I hope it may be of interest to many who love the Western Isles. My first aim has been to provide the most correct text from a careful collation of the surviving MSS.[1]; with the gathering together of what is known of the author, some picture emerges of the little-known See of the Isles as he knew it, and of the Church in the Highlands which he served after the Reformation; while as to the Islands themselves, I have reviewed their condition in the light of what he tells us, with occasional glimpses from other

[1] A note on these is given at pp. 148-50. See also p. 45.

sources, and have pursued Hume Brown's attempt to identify all the islands named by Monro with some additional success. I have also sought to bring out the value of the 'Genealogies', which have been largely neglected in previous editions.

My thanks are due, and gladly acknowledged, to all those who have helped me in this task. Particularly I would mention the Trustees of the National Library of Scotland and their staff, through whom I have had access to the three copies of Monro's manuscript in their care. The patience and courtesy of the staff of the Edinburgh Central Library, as I followed my quest through many byways, have never failed. And I am grateful to the Society of Antiquaries of Scotland for permission to consult a copy of the manuscript in their keeping. I should like also to thank all those who have encouraged me by putting their professional learning at my disposal in a field where history, topography and philology meet, and many friends and acquaintances in the Hebrides and elsewhere who have made my travels in time and space as pleasant as I hope they may have been profitable. To four in particular I wish to offer special thanks—to Dr C. T. McInnes, of the Scottish Record Office, for help in locating and deciphering records, and for some assistance with the manuscript; to Dr Gordon Donaldson, of the University of Edinburgh, for many helpful suggestions regarding the biography of Donald Monro; to Dr A. B. Taylor, now Registrar-General for Scotland, for advice about place-names and other topographical matters; and to Mr J. L. Campbell of Canna, who generously put at my disposal (through the good offices of Professor W. Croft Dickinson) an article on some of the lesser islands mentioned by Monro.

In case it should be thought that I have relied too much on books, manuscripts and records, I should add that light has often been shed on these authorities by a personal knowledge of many of the Islands described by Monro. I have not yet visited them all, but I like to think that I was following in his footsteps when I stood in the ruined palace of the Lords of the Isles in Islay, on the Council Isle of Finlaggan, and among the tombs of the kings in Iona; that he had scrambled before me up the sea-cliff which is the only access to the Pigmies' Isle at the Butt of Lewis; and that he too may have felt that the cormorants which stand sentinel on the rocks of Cairn na Burgh Mor were jeering at his attempts to make a landing on the most ' unwinnable ' of the Treshnish Isles.

It has pleased me to think that, after a lapse of four centuries, I might be doing justice to a fellow-clansman from my own native parish of Kiltearn. I hope that in its new form his little book may prove more attractive, and even more useful, than it has been in the past.

INVERNESS R. W. M.

CONTENTS

* * *

INTRODUCTION

1. THE ISLANDS

During the turbulent years when Mary Queen of Scots was a child, the Hebrides, or Western Isles of Scotland, appear in history as the scene of almost incessant clan warfare or rebellion. There was no powerful authority to take the place of the forfeited Lords of the Isles; and, while heirs to that great house remained as a centre of disaffection, and rival parties disputed for the central government, Henry VIII was busy meddling in Scottish affairs, and the warring chiefs were open to the influence of wider ambitions.

Such a background lends a deeper interest to the account left us by Donald Monro, which presents a picture of the islands from the inside. It is the earliest known description which is plainly from the pen of one who knew them; it forms the basis of the account of that region given by Buchanan in his Latin *History of Scotland*; and, while many details remain untold and forgotten, a study of Monro's *Description* reveals much that would otherwise be lost about conditions in the Hebrides four hundred years ago.

We find the castles of the island chiefs still dominating the landscape, with the churches, chapels and religious houses of the pre-Reformation Church taking a more modest, but still considerable, place. The chase ranks as the most popular pastime, and simple husbandry as the chief occupation of the people. Of their homes and home life we learn little, and of their numbers nothing; but it is clear that the islands were more fully stocked and cultivated than they are today, and that fewer of them were uninhabited. Superstition was not yet dead, although the old tales which find notice in his pages are treated by Monro with becoming caution.

Living in the days when the chiefs made war upon each other in the manner of independent princes, Monro is particular to name the castles in each island which still gave shelter to their lords. Skye had five of them, Mull three, and there were two in Islay, besides the 'palace' of the old Lords of the Isles. Monro also mentions the rude sea-girt fortresses of Cairn na Burgh Mor in the Treshnish group, 'easily made unwynable be craftie men', Kisimul Castle in Barra, and the less well-known Dun Chonuill off the coast of Lorne. But stout walls and surrounding water were not always a sure protection, for in an Islay loch there was a castle which used to belong to the Clan Donald of Kintyre, but in Monro's day was usurped by Maclean of Duart; while the fair isle of Gigha, of which a Macneil should have been laird, belonged to the Macdonalds. That ownership was constantly changing is clear from other sources also: Rum, for example, although the property of Maclean of Coll, 'obeyis to M^c^gillane of Doward instantlie' (*i.e.* at present), according to Monro's account, but a report prepared soon afterwards says it 'is possesst and in the handis of Clan-Ranald'. There is a wealth of significance, too, in the kirk where 'M^c^cloyd of Leozus uses to dwell, quhan he wald be quiet or feirit', on an island in the mouth of Loch Roag facing the Atlantic.[1]

From Monro we can learn also something of the religious buildings of his day, in spite of a carping critic who remarked that 'if he had been Verger instead of Dean, he could not have been much more ignorant of the diocese to which he belonged'. He mentions that the Isle of Man and Iona were once the seat of the Bishops of the Isles, as Lismore was for Argyll, although it is true that he says nothing of their cathedrals. He provides us, however, with the only surviving description of the tombs of the kings in Iona, before they disappeared, and the earliest reference to the

[1] Skene, iii 434, *s.v.* 'Romb'. See note A: Island Castles (p. 120). A detailed list of sources will be found on pages 148-58.

old church of St Clement at Rodil, in Harris, an architectural gem which survived the Reformation. There were two monasteries in Iona (one of monks, the other of nuns), one 'of chanons' in Oronsay (near Colonsay), and another 'which is decayed' of friars on Holy Island, off Arran. He also lists the parish churches and many of the chapels scattered throughout the diocese, and states which of the islands then belonged to the Bishop and to the Abbot and Prioress of Iona.[2]

Of the people who lived in the islands, Monro gives only passing glimpses, but from his account we can build up some picture of the life they led. Most of the island lords are named only by title or patronymic, such as 'my Lord of Argile', 'Donald Gormesoun' and 'M^{c}kenzie', but in a few cases he is more explicit. It has been pointed out that, while he was eulogising the 'bluid' of the Stewarts of Bute, their chief was being summoned before Parliament for devastating the islands of Arran and Bute, and demolishing the castle of Brodick. Many of the great chiefs in those days held by force of arms lands which rightly belonged to the Church, and an ecclesiastic must have looked askance at such usurpation. Monro's most-quoted comment refers to Raasay and Rona, both 'perteining to M^{c}gillichallum of Raarsay be the sword, & to the Bischop of the Iles in heritage'. The southern isles of Barra—still sometimes known as 'the Bishop's Isles'—had also passed out of the hands of the Church, and the national records provide evidence of an action brought by the Bishop against both Macneil of Barra and Macleod of Raasay for their remissness in paying dues to the island See.[3]

When the Church was thus despoiled of her lands by the leading men, and they themselves sometimes lived in fear of their lives, it is small wonder that there were lawless characters among the people. Thieves and cut-throats

[2] See note B: Religious Houses (p. 125).
[3] McArthur, 166. See note C: The Bishop's Isles (p. 128).

lurked in the woods of islands now destitute of trees, and even in holes underground among the heather. No glossary is needed to explain the menace of South Rona (where part of the harbour is still called *Port nan Robaireann*), which then afforded a haven for ' ruggaris & reevaris till await upon the pailing & spuilzeing of poor mens geir '.[4]

Statements such as these by men of responsibility, says a modern historian of Skye, would no doubt convey exaggerated notions of the disorderliness that prevailed in the Isles, and they explain the extravagant accounts that were subsequently written by men who knew the Highlands only by repute. It is perhaps more surprising, however, that Monro gives us comparatively few glimpses of this darker side of the picture, which led the late Canon MacLeod to liken the Highlands of that period to a second Cave of Adullam, to which there resorted ' every one that was in distress, and every one that was in debt, and every one that was discontented '. During the first half of the sixteenth century, he pointed out, in addition to three full-scale rebellions, six clan feuds were in progress. Canon MacLeod did not think that the ' silence ' of Monro and the few other writers of the day whose accounts have come down to us is any proof that the terrible conditions which he describes did not in fact exist. But this was, after all, also a time when art flourished in the Isles—a sculptured tomb still to be seen on Oronsay, for example, represents the prior who reigned there at the time of Monro's tour of the diocese —and Monro gives great prominence to the peaceful pursuits followed in most of the islands. His account has, indeed, led Hume Brown and another historian of our own day, the late Mr W. C. Mackenzie, to describe this as the Golden Age of the Isles.[5]

[4] Nicolson's *Skye*, 432. Monro's ' ruggaris and reevaris ' have found their way into Jamieson's *Dictionary* and R. B. Cunninghame Graham's *Notes on the District of Menteith* (3rd edn., 1906, 12).

[5] Nicolson's *Skye*, 97. MacLeod, 80-1, 85, 87. P. Hume Brown, *Scotland in the Time of Queen Mary* (1904), 30. Mackenzie (1937), 126.

The chase was popular, and we learn from Monro of the 'fair hunting games' which were enjoyed in Islay, Mull, Skye and Harris. Deer were plentiful, but instead of present-day stalking methods great hunts called 'tynchells' were organised in Monro's time, for which an isthmus like that between the two Lochs Tarbert in Jura was specially convenient. Other game mentioned include otters, martins and the humble rabbit; the slaughter of seals in the Ascrib Isles and Haskeir is reported, and on the sandbanks of Loch Gruinard in Islay seals were slain with the help of dogs trained for the purpose; catching the wild sheep on the Flannan Isles seems also from Monro's account to have been a sport in itself. He is particular to list the islands where the falcon nested, for hawking in those days was important enough to find its way into Acts of Parliament, and the royal falconer visited the Isles to secure the birds reserved for the King. From his remark that there were no wolves in Harris, it may be surmised that they were to be found on some of the other islands.[6]

Scattered throughout Monro's *Description* are many observations on the husbandry of the islands in his day. One does not gather that horses were common or greatly valued from the few references to them which he makes; and perhaps he allows his opinion of their use in agriculture to slip out in his notice of Taransay, where 'all the tilth is delved with spades, except so much as a horse plough will till; and yet they have abundance of barley, and plenty corn'. In Harris there was twice as much delved land as there was tilled, and the same comparison is made in other islands. Cattle and sheep, on the other hand, were much more common, and probably on many of the islands did not call for mention; even in remote North Rona, 50 miles north of Lewis, there were so many that they not only kept the inhabitants supplied with meat, but also paid most of their rent. In several of the islands the sheep ran wild on

[6] See note D: Island Sports (p. 129).

the hills; the Soay breed on St Kilda were remarkable for their size and length of tail, and those on the Flannans had flesh so ' wild gusted ' that it ' may not be eaten by honest and clean men for fatness '. Pigs, against which there was a Celtic prejudice, are hardly mentioned, and never directly as part of the produce of the Isles; nor is there any reference to poultry—to which a similar objection was taken—although we know from other sources that they formed part of the rent of several of the islands in Monro's day.[7]

Monro says nothing about the climate of the Isles. Of crops there was not much variety, but innumerable references to corn and grass show that the islands were by no means bare. It is possible that the soil has become less productive than it was in the old days when there were more cattle on the ground. The two most common phrases in Monro's account are ' inhabite & manurit ' (*i.e.* cultivated) and ' fertile & frutfull '; and in the case of two islands in Loch Roag (one of them Great Bernera, where there has recently been some talk of evacuation) both expressions are used together to emphasise their fertility. The type of crop is not often specified, but Bute and Skye were fertile ' namelie for aittis ' (especially for oats); bear, or barley, is the only other kind of crop named, and even in North Rona, where natural clover abounded, there was ' such fair white barley meal made like flour '. Only the Flannan Isles are described as being ' nather manurit nor inhabite ', and lonely Sula Sgeir (where the men of Ness used to go for wild fowl even in those far-off days) was ' without grass or heather '. Among the trees found in the islands the birch, the hazel, and the yew are named, and there were also thorns and elders. Raasay had ' two fair orchards ', one at either castle, and MacLeod of Lewis had another on an island in Loch Erisort, which the gardener had free for his services.

Monro's references to fishing are of interest. A great

[7] Cumming, 129-30, 369. Pennant, i 254-5. Skene, iii 429, 430, 432, 435, 437, *s.v.* Lewis, Harris, Skye, Mull, Islay.

part of the rents and revenues of the Bishopric of the Isles used to consist in the teind of herring and other fish, but it has been held by some writers that very little fishing was done by the West Highlanders in the early days. The *Description* is full of references to the excellent harbours among the islands, although not all those mentioned as suitable for 'Highland galleys' are now fit even for fishing boats. In the sea, lochs and rivers there was 'gud tak' of herring, salmon, white fish, whiting, haddock and 'pintill fish' (perhaps the pipe fish). In Lewis there was a cove where whitings and haddocks could be caught by hook and line, and in Loch Bee (South Uist) many varieties of fish were caught in a dyke which separated it from the sea. Monro's mention of 'murens' being found in Fuday in the Barra Isles has given rise to some speculation, and earned him a passage in the Scots dictionary of Dr Jamieson, who suggested that lampreys might be meant, although he thought conger eels more probable. An unusual kind of fish caught in Loch Bee—the size and shape of a salmon, with no scales, white underneath and black above, with fins like a salmon—may have been the coalfish. Whales were sometimes caught, particularly in Lewis, where as many as 27 were once taken.[8]

Apart from agriculture and fishing, Monro says little of industry in the islands. In Belnahua and 'Slait' (perhaps Ellanbeich, now quarried out of existence) 'there is abundance of slates to be won'; lead ore was to be found in Lismore and Islay, and Raasay was 'full of freestone and good quarries'. Among the Outer Isles, where the absence of peat still causes inconvenience, Monro reports plenty of fuel in Great Bernera and Vacsay, but Monach was 'not well fyrit'; while in Lewis itself 'the place where he wins his peats this year, there he sows his bear the next year: after that he manures it well with sea-ware'. There is, of

[8] Skene, iii 430, 431-2, 433, *s.v.* Harris, St Kilda, Skye. MacLeod, 61-2. *A.P.S.*, vii 386. See note D (p. 129).

course, no great kelp industry, but Monro mentions seaweed as abounding in Little Bernera.

Of the homes and home-life of the people Monro unfortunately tells us nothing in his *Description*, although he may have supplied Buchanan with the details with which he prefaced his Latin version of it. Even on spiritual matters he merely says that the inhabitants of St Kilda are ‘ simple creatures, scant learned in any religion ’, while the ‘ simple people ’ of North Rona are also ‘ scant of any religion ’. A chaplain, he says, accompanied MacLeod's steward to the former at midsummer each year, but in his absence they baptised their children themselves.

Superstition, and what we would regard today as beliefs not far removed from it, provide three curious tales, which have earned Monro the ridicule of some later writers. When any man died in North Rona, ‘ as the ancients of that country allege ’ (adds the cautious churchman), they left a spade and a shovel in St Ronan's chapel, and on the morrow they found the place of the grave marked with a spade. In a spring on the top of a hill on Barra—again ‘ as alleged by the ancient countrymen ’—cockles were formed in embryo, and carried down by the stream to the Traigh Mor, where they grew into large cockles; of this story, which successive ministers of Barra have been at pains to refute, Monro leaves the confirmation to the historian Hector Boece, who had a similar tale about a spring in Mull. Perhaps the strangest legend of all is that of the Pigmies' Isle near the Butt of Lewis, where there was a little kirk under the floor of which were buried ‘ certain bones and round heads of wonderful little quantity, alleged to be the bones of the said pigmies, which may be likely ’—but (adds Monro, cautious as ever) ‘ I leave this far of it to the ancients of Lewis ’. This island and its cell have been rediscovered in our own day.[9]

But it is with fact rather than fancy that Monro sets out

[9] See notes E and F : Barra ‘ Cockles ’, The Pigmies' Isle (pp. 131, 133).

to deal. Of 250 odd islands which he lists, more than 220 can be identified with reasonable certainty, and a few more are to be found on the older maps; the remainder are unrecognisable today under the names he gives them. Starting with the Isle of Man in the south—it used to be more closely associated with the Hebrides than it is now—and extending over 300 miles to Sula Sgeir in the northern seas, Monro's *Description* ranges from great islands such as Lewis and Skye to little rocks like Eilean a' Bhealaich (between Scarba and Lunga) and the Small Isles of Jura. Some are named in a confusing order, and he seems to know of several groups only by hearsay. His frequent over-estimate of distances between the islands suggests that Monro was not experienced in judging distances at sea, but on land his measurements are in most cases astonishingly accurate. Keeping in mind that his computations were made in Scots miles, of which there were only nine to ten miles south of the Border, one finds few serious discrepancies. The dimensions of Arran are indeed much exaggerated, no doubt because of the mountainous interior, and he makes Bute and Raasay too short, and Rum too long; but his estimates of the much greater lengths of Jura, Mull, Skye, the Uists and Lewis and Harris will be found not far off the mark.[10]

Regarding the names of islands, and the other place-names scattered through his work, Monro's reputation has been allowed to suffer through the errors of copyists to whom Gaelic was probably unknown. This will be seen by comparing the text now printed with that on which previous editions are based. In the former the spellings are much nearer to Buchanan's, and they are also more consistent with one another; although Monro's acquaintance with Gaelic was slight, Buchanan is known to have been familiar with it: 'having met, when in France, with a woman who was said to be possessed with a devil, and who professed to speak all languages, he accosted her in Gaelic. As neither

[10] See Appendix II : Identifying the Islands (p. 111).

she nor her familiar returned any answer, he entered a protest that the devil was ignorant of that language'. In Monro's 'Kerveray' there is an echo of the *bh* of which Professor Watson noted a still distinct trace in the local pronunciation of Kerrera; 'Colvansay' is nearer to the modern Gaelic '*Colbhasa*' and the original Norse '*Kolbeins-ey*' than the now standard 'Colonsay' or the 'Colnansay' of the previous editions; and Dr MacBain has shown that Monro's 'Raarsay' is more than an oddity of his own. On the rare occasions when Monro hazarded a derivation for a place-name, as in Skye and Jura, he has had the approval of modern scholars, and here again the present text proves a surer guide.[11]

There can be no doubt that Monro had first-hand knowledge of many of the islands which he describes. Personal references are few, but there are enough to prove this fact beyond dispute. In writing of Harris, he says 'when I was there'; he admits to having been among those who dug for bones ('and I myself among the lave') at the Pigmies' Isle—and he must have been a fair cragsman if he reached its summit without assistance; his detailed account of Loch Bee indicates a personal acquaintance with South Uist; his statement that 'there is not a fairer and more profitable sands for cockles in any part of the world' suggests that he had relished the cockles of Barra; and he evidently examined the supposed embryo cockles there himself; while his account of the tombs of the kings on Iona is so circumstantial that he must surely have examined them himself.

Long after Monro's day, to have visited some of the islands he describes gave the traveller a claim to distinction scarcely less than to have explored the sources of the Nile or the Niger.[12] It is natural, therefore, to ask: Who was this High Dean of the Isles whose *Description* is the earliest that has come down to us?

[11] See note G: Place Names (p. 134). [12] MacCulloch (1819), i 204.

2. THE AUTHOR[1]

Donald Monro was born about the beginning of the sixteenth century, and he was related to several of the most influential familes in the Highlands and Islands of Scotland. His father Alexander, who held the lands of Kiltearn beside the Cromarty Firth from his Chief, was the son of Hugh Munro of Coul and grandson of George Munro of Foulis, who was killed in 1452. From their founder, the Kiltearn family were known as *Sliochd Alastair mhic Uistean*, and marriage relationships have been traced with the Macdonalds of Glengarry, Sleat and Islay, and with the Macleods of Lewis. Of Alexander himself little is known, beyond the fact that he married Janet, daughter of Farquhar Maclean of the Dochgarroch line, known as the 'Macleans of the North'; this Farquhar was closely connected with, if he was not the same person as, the Bishop of the Isles of that name who held the See from 1530-44.[2]

Monro thus had early associations with the Western Isles; his family also had a tradition of service in the Church. The Laird of Kiltearn had six sons, and while the lands passed to the younger of them, the eldest (Donald) adopted the Church as his career. In this he followed two of his uncles—Mr John Monro of Balconie, who had graduated at the University of Aberdeen, and became Vicar of Urquhart; and Sir Donald Monro, who was Provost of the Collegiate Church of Tain. No doubt family influence played its part in determining the appointments held by

[1] The chief published notices of Monro are in *Fasti* (1870), Ross (1884), Brown (1893), Mackenzie (1898), Smith (1909), and Beveridge (1911); for details see p. 150. Dr Gordon Donaldson has made many useful suggestions for this section, particularly regarding the immediately post-Reformation period.

[2] Allan MS. *Chron. Acc.*, 27, 28, where Donald is called 'Mr John [*sic*] Munro who was Archdean of the Isles superintendent of Ross and minister of Killtearn'. Fraser-Mackintosh, ii 39-40. Mackenzie's *Munros*, 350, 359, 410. For Munros (or Monros) of Kiltearn see 'A Kiltearn Family' [by R.W.M.] in *Ross-shire Journal*, 5 Jan. 1951.

the younger Donald, for we first hear of him as being presented in 1526 to the vicarage of Snizort and Raasay, in Skye. This parish was in the diocese of Sodor or the Isles, and formed part of the Bishop's heritage; but a considerable portion, according to Monro himself, was held by the Macleods of Raasay 'by the sword'. Monro's relative, Donald Maclean of Dochgarroch, later became at least nominal proprietor of Raasay and part of Trotternish, and he may have been given these lands by the Bishop with the object of expelling the usurpers.[3]

All Scotland was then passing through a century of trouble and disturbance. Monro's presentation to Raasay was made in the name of the captive boy-king James V, during whose minority the usual struggle for power was carried on by the great nobles of the land. On reaching man's estate, however, James did much to strengthen the influence of the central government, and his fleet was seen off Raasay in 1540 during one of his personal visits made to overawe the island chiefs. But he refused to follow Henry VIII's example in throwing off allegiance to the Pope, and when his early death in 1542 left his daughter Mary—a girl a few days old—as successor to the Scottish throne, the English king saw a chance to interfere in the affairs of his northern neighbours. In the turmoil which ensued, the island chiefs rose in rebellion under Donald Dubh, who assumed the forefeited title of Lord of the Isles, and Henry did his utmost to wean them from their Scottish allegiance. The 'Council of the Isles' was revived, and in 1545 a fleet was gathered in the Hebrides, and actually set out to

[3] *Chron. Acc.*, 28. *R.P.S.*, i 534 (3524). Dowden's *Church*, 113-14. Fraser-Mackintosh, ii 39-40. Mackenzie's *Macleods*, 345—but his *Munros* omits the 1526 presentation. For uncle John see Mackenzie's *Munros*, 343; *Exchequer Rolls*, xvii 668; *R.M.S.*, iv 117 (508). For uncle Donald see Mackenzie's *Munros*, 410, amended and amplified by *Foulis Writs*, 12, 14, 17, 21, 24 (41, 46, 57, 73, 84); *R.M.S.*, ii 544 (2380); *R.P.S.*, ii 582 (3870); *Exchequer Rolls*, xvi 207, xvii 669; *Cawdor*, 150, 162; *Mackintosh Muniments* (1903), 18 (50); *O.P.S.*, ii (i) 417-19, 584, 585.

cooperate with the English party; but with the death of Donald Dubh, and the severe measures taken against the rebels, a general pacification of the Highlands and Islands seems to have been accomplished by degrees.[4]

These events had their effect on the Church, and through it on Donald Monro. The Bishopric of the Isles was the most scattered, and also one of the poorest, in the pre-Reformation Church of Scotland. It comprised all the islands off the western coast—the *Sudreyar* of the Norse chronicles—and was originally based on the Isle of Man. With the conquest of Man by the English and the Papal schism—when England and Scotland acknowledged different Popes—however, a separate See of 'Sodor and Man' had arisen as part of the province of York, and the Scottish portion of the bishopric had to find a new headquarters. As Monro himself says, the Abbey of Icolmkill or Iona was the Cathedral Church of the Bishops of the Isles 'sen the time thai were banist out of the Ile of man be the Inglismen', and the arrangement was authorised by the Pope in 1498. Thereafter the Abbacy of Iona was held with the Bishopric, the occupant of the See thus being Bishop of the Isles and perpetual Commendator of the monastery. Thirteen Hebridean islands, and one islet, are mentioned by Monro as pertaining to the Bishop in property; but the share-out of Church lands among the local chiefs had already begun, and even in Bishop Farquhar's day it was complained that the revenues were difficult to collect. Although the 'Bishop's Isles' to the south of Barra retained that name long afterwards—and Barra Head is sometimes known as '*Bearnaraidh an Easbuig*' to this day—it would be little consolation to their titular lord. A contemporary of Monro's says that the Bishops had their 'principall dwelling places' on Iona; but what a later visitor believed to have been the Bishop's residence, or palace, was 'certainly very

[4] Gregory, esp. 172 and note, 179. For Council of the Isles, see Appendix I (p. 95).

mean'; the ruins (still standing to the north of the church) consisted of 'a large hall open to the roof, a chamber I suppose he used a ladder to get into, and under the chamber a buttery; the roof is now fallen in. I believe the offices were without, according to the custom of the country'.[5]

Just as the Bishop's palace was allowed to decay, so it was soon forgotten 'quhat or how manye dignities wes in that sea and quha wes the memberis of that chaptoure'; perhaps, indeed, there was no chapter, for the loss of Man would naturally leave the diocese with many imperfections. Even the neighbouring diocese of Argyll, based on Lismore, was considered so remote, and its people so wild and uncivilised, that few churchmen aspired to become its Bishop. In the Isles, where the power of the Macleans had risen on the ruins of the old Lordship, more than one member of that clan was appointed to the episcopal office. In 1544, Bishop Farquhar obtained licence to resign the See into the hands of the Pope in favour of Roderick Maclean, then Archdeacon of the Isles. The promotion of the latter was opposed by the island chiefs, who supported the claims of Ruari, Dean of Morven, brother of the Captain of Clanranald, and one of the two plenipotentiaries sent by the Council of the Isles to treat with Henry VIII; the other envoy—Patrick Maclean, brother of the Laird of Duart, Bailie of Icolmkill and Justiciar of the Isles—was granted the temporality of the diocese and the Abbacy of Iona in 1547, until a Bishop should be provided. Archdeacon Roderick was confirmed as Bishop of the Isles in March 1550; but Patrick, with his brother's assistance, occupied and held the Abbey, and as late as January 1552 we find

[5] *O.P.S.*, ii (i) 291-2, 294. Innes (1860), xxxi. W. J. Duncan, note in Wodrow's *Collections*, 472. *H.P.*, i 83. Dowden's *Church*, 58. 'Rentale of Bischopis landis within the Illis' (1561) in Iona Club, 3-4; Maclean, 66-7; Gordon, 96. *Thirds*, xiv and note. Sacheverell, 103. Pennant, i 294. Walcott, 166, plan opp. 201. Trenholme, 117-18. Ritchie, map. Skene, iii 436. For the Bishop's Isles, see note C (p. 128).

the Privy Council ordering him to deliver Iona to the new Bishop.[6]

These competing claims, reflected in the national records, make it difficult to trace the career of Donald Monro with exactness. It has even been suggested that the title ' High Dean of the Isles ', which he added to his name, may have had no more significance than those scoffed at in Sir David Lindsay's contemporary verses:—

> The pure Priest thynkis he gettis no rycht,
> Be he nocht stylit lyke ane knycht,
> And callit Schir, affore his name,
> As Schir Thomas, and Schir Wilyame.
> *All monkrye, ye may heire and se,*
> *Ar callit Denis, for dignitie;*
> Quhowbeit his mother mylk the kow,
> He mone be callit Dene Androw,
> Dene Peter, Dene Paull, and Dene Robart.

It is clear, however, that Monro styled himself ' Sir Donald ' merely because that was the usual designation in those days for a priest who had not studied at a University or obtained a degree (and there is no evidence of his having followed his uncle as a student to Aberdeen); while to use the specific title ' High Dean of the Isles ' was a very different matter from calling himself ' Dean Donald '.[7]

But there are stronger grounds for believing that this territorial office was more than one of Lindsay's paper deaneries. It is recorded in the Register of the Privy Seal that, on 2nd March 1548 (according to the old calendar,

[6] *A.P.S.*, iv 554-5. Theiner, 608 (1047). *R.P.S.*, iii 155, 382-3 (977, 2367). Keith, 307. Dowden's *Bishops*, 292, 390. Gregory, 172 and note. Hannay, 610, 614. *Clan Donald*, i 379, 380.

[7] Lyndsay, 3rd book, line 4666 &c. *D.N.B.*, xiii 629. Jamieson, iii 525-7, *s.v.* Pope's Knights. The only reference to Monro as High Dean of the Isles is in the title of his ' Geneologies ' (see p. 92) and *Bal.* and *Macf.* MSS. of ' Description '.

which began the year on 25th March, it was still 1547), 'Master Archibald [*sic*] Munro, chaplain' was presented in the name of Queen Mary to the Archdeaconry of the Isles, when it should become vacant by the demission of 'the venerable clerk Master Roderick Maclean'; four years later (as we shall see) the name of 'Sr Donald Monroy, archdeane of the ilis' appears in a document which still survives; and he is later on record as 'archidiaconus Insularum'. There is no other trace of a sixteenth century priest named Master Archibald Munro or Monro, and indeed that Christian name was not in use in the clan at that time; Donald Monro is not appointed by any other order under the Privy Seal: and it is therefore reasonable to presume that he became Archdeacon on the elevation of Roderick Maclean to the Bishopric. Most of the Scottish dioceses were divided into rural deaneries, and there is a Dean of Mull on record in 1532. 'Archdean' is often used in our records in place of the proper title 'Archdeacon'; and as the functions of the latter made him in reality the 'chief of the Deans', it is not unnatural—although the style is not otherwise known—that Monro's office should be Englished into the title of 'High Dean of the Isles'.[8]

One of the new Archdeacon's first actions was to make himself familiar with his diocese, and he accordingly travelled through many of the islands in 1549. As the 'Bishop's eye' (*oculus episcopi*), Monro would have the supervision of all the parochial clergy within his bounds, with the duty of visiting its churches and the right to be received and entertained in the manses. Whether the

[8] *R.P.S.*, iii 424 (2660), original examined in H.M. Register House, Edinburgh. Bond of Sep. 1553, preserved in Register House in Richmond and Gordon Collection, box 13, bundle 7, no. 21; not previously cited in notices of Monro, as 'Monroy' was incorrectly deciphered as 'Mourray' in *Spalding Misc.*, iv 22, quoted *S.H.R.*, xxiv 173. *Foulis Writs*, 23 (78). *R.M.S.*, iv 330 (1455, 1456). *Cawdor*, 158. Grub, i 278 note. Sir (otherwise Master) Richard Lawson was Archdeacon of the Isles in Jan. 1540-1 (Hannay, 499); the office fell into disuetude 'by remoteness of the place and iniquity of the latter tymes', but was revived in 1662 (*A.P.S.*, vii 403; Craven, 109).

writing of his famous *Description* was one of the objects of the tour of inspection cannot now be ascertained. Such an array of place-names, and such a wealth of detail, could only be gathered by a man on the spot, although no doubt his clergy would assist him with information about the islands which he could not visit in person. At least the outline must have been committed to paper while the extraordinary ramifications of the island See were fresh in his memory. That literary interests were not unknown even in remote island churches is proved by the valuable collection of Gaelic poetry made by Sir James MacGregor, Monro's contemporary as Dean of Lismore. It was probably at the same time that Monro collected the material for his *Geneologies of the Cheiff Clans of the Iles*, in which he recorded the descent of the five main branches of the Clan Donald—Sleat, Islay and Kintyre, Clanranald and Glengarry, Clanian of Ardnamurchan, and the Lochaber Macdonalds.[9]

Monro's office, added to his family connections, would place him in a position of commanding influence. When the Bishop himself was absent from the diocese, he would be the most important clerical figure in the Hebrides. Bishop Roderick only held the See of the Isles for some four years, and his successor is unlikely to have taken any very deep interest in so remote and scattered a diocese. Alexander Gordon, brother of the Earl of Huntly, had been consoled for his failure to secure the Archbishopric of Glasgow by the high-sounding but empty title of Archbishop of Athens, with the promise of the first See to fall vacant; and so,

[9] Dowden's *Church*, 218-21. Carmichael's *Lismore*, esp. 110-17. The only authorities for Monro's journey are the title of his 'Description' (p. 46) and Buchanan's reference (p. 42); the date 1549 is given in Balfour's 1642 MS. That Monro did not visit all the islands is suggested in Appendix II (p. 112). The Bishop and Archdeacon of Lismore—but not those of the Isles—attended a Provincial Synod held by the Prelates and Clergy of Scotland at Edinburgh on 27 Nov. 1549 (*Statutes of the Scottish Church, 1225-1559*, ed. David Patrick, Sco. Hist. Soc., Edin. 1907, pp. 85-8).

when Bishop Roderick died in 1553, Gordon was provided to the poor See of the Isles. Perhaps Monro's *Description*, which hardly touches on ecclesiastical matters except to name the islands which pertained to the Bishop, was prepared for his benefit, as the Macleans who preceded him would scarcely need information from a subordinate about the Hebrides. However that may be, the new Bishop soon contrived to have himself transferred to the See of Galloway. John Campbell, a son of the house of Cawdor, is mentioned as Bishop-elect of the Isles in 1558 and 1560, but the See was one of the two which were vacant at the Reformation.[10]

Whether the Archdeacon had his headquarters in Iona, and resided there, it is not possible to say. In the very year of the journey through the Isles, and again in 1552 (at Ardersier) and 1554 (at the Cathedral Church of Ross), a Sir Donald Monro witnessed documents as parson of Y; this has been identified as Eye, in Lewis, one of the parsonages attached to the Bishopric of the Isles, but the name is also one of the early forms used for Iona. Also in 1552, he was presented to the vacant rectory of Uig, in the Trotternish district of Skye, which looks like an example of the pluralism against which the Reformers were inveighing. At Ruthven in Badenoch, in September 1553, 'Sir Donald Monroy, archdeane of the ilis' was guiding the pen of John Moydertach, Captain of Clanranald, when he and his son promised 'to keype guid rewill' within their territories by a bond entered into with Huntly, then Lieutenant-General in the North; other witnesses included Huntly's brother Alexander (not yet provided to the Isles), and his son George, Lord Gordon. Monro clung to his title even after the Reformation, for as late as January 1563, when he witnessed two charters regarding an exchange of lands in Ross and Sutherland between Munro of Foulis and Bayne

[10] Wodrow's *Collections*, 141, 477. *A.P.S.*, ii 525, 603*a*, 606. Keith, 307. Dowden's *Bishops*, 292. Innes (1847), xvi. Craven, 18-27. Donaldson, 353.

of Tullich, we still find him styled Archdeacon of the Isles.[11]

* * *

Although 1560 forms a natural landmark in tracing the career of any churchman of the period, the Reformation was not the product of a single year. The growing degeneracy and corruption of the old Church, and the gradual advance of the new faith, had an earlier origin; similarly, the old form of religion was not overthrown in a night, and the new system of Church government was many years in growing to full stature. Thus Monro was a young man when the first martyr of the Reformation, Patrick Hamilton, was burned at the stake; and he was full of years when the influence of Andrew Melville, the firm opponent of episcopacy in all its forms, began to be felt in Scotland.[12]

It was in 1560, however, that the new Confession of Faith was adopted, and the Reformers were able to start purging the Church of some of its abuses. Compromise helped to smooth the path, for all persons in possession of benefices continued to enjoy their fruits with the exception of one-third, which was to be collected to augment the revenues of the crown and pay stipends to the Reformed clergy. Scotland was divided into ten dioceses or districts —the Isles were to be shared between Ross and Argyll— over each of which a Superintendent (answerable to the General Assembly, which met twice a year) was to be appointed. The Bishops of Galloway, Orkney, Caithness and Argyll supported the Reformation, and all of them, except perhaps the last, took part in the work of the Reformed Church. This was the course adopted by the

[11] *Foulis Writs*, 18, 23, 32 (61, 78, 105). *R.M.S.*, iv 168, 330 (750, 1455, 1456). Calendar of Register House Charters (unpublished), no. 1629. *R.P.S.*, iv 290 (1791); *O.P.S.*, ii (i) 354, and see 381. Bond of Sept. 1553 (see note 8 p. 16). John Mackay, 100. Mackenzie (1903), 521. Fraser-Mackintosh, i 125. Mackenzie's *Munros*, 46.

[12] Hamilton was burned at the stake in 1528, and Melville returned to Scotland in 1574.

Archdeacon of the Isles, whose Chief and cousin, Robert *Mor* Munro of Foulis, must have been among the first in the Highlands to accept the new beliefs. Henry Sinclair, the conservative Bishop of Ross (who was more a lawyer than a churchman), had been permitted to retire to France, where he died a few years later; but among those who conformed were his Archdeacon (Donald Fraser), the Provost of the Collegiate Church of Tain (Nicholas Ross), and several of the lesser clergy of the diocese.[13]

Donald Monro was not one of those who were declared fully qualified for the ministry by the Reformation Assembly of 1560, but he was admitted soon afterwards to the charge of Kiltearn, which was probably his native parish. As the young Church became more fully organised, three, four, or even a greater number of neighbouring churches were placed under one minister, with the assistance of a 'reader' in each parish. This was especially necessary in the Highlands, where manpower was short, and Monro's charge was later extended to include also Lemlair (the western and smaller portion of the present parish of Kiltearn) and Alness. The manses of these three parishes used to stand within the precincts of the Cathedral Church of Ross at Fortrose, but according to tradition Monro lived at Castle Craig, a former residence of the Bishops of Ross on the south side of the Cromarty Firth, facing Kiltearn. He is said to have crossed the Firth by boat on Sundays to preach at his three churches in succession, and the turf-covered ruins of Cladh Mo-Brigh—where the old church of Lemlair stood—on the shore about two miles east of Dingwall are pointed out as the first spot in Ross-shire where the doctrines of the Reformed religion were expounded.[14]

[13] Knox, ii 291-5. Dowden's *Bishops*, 228, 250, 268, 375. Donaldson, 351, 354. *Fasti* (new edn.), vii 1-76 *passim*, esp. 10, 70. Some clergy in Argyll and the Isles also submitted to the measures of Reformation in 1560, including Robert Montgomery, Archdeacon of Lismore (Craven, 14-16).

[14] *Stat. Acc.*, i 293, 298. *O.P.S.*, ii (ii) 580-1. Watson (1904), 85, and (1924), 93, 94. Wodrow *Misc.*, i 326. Noble, 76.

It was not long before Donald Monro became prominent in the higher councils of the Reformers, who had their own special difficulties in the Highlands. When the fifth General Assembly met in December 1562, it was complained 'that the north countrie, for the most part, was destitute of ministers'. Men suitable for the post of Superintendent were rare, and their salaries (some £500 to £700 each) were a heavy burden on the Church. John Carswell, Superintendent of Argyll—who later became Bishop of Argyll and the Isles—was the only one appointed for the Highland area. Successive Assemblies therefore granted commissions 'to endure only for a year', which gave certain ministers the power of Superintendents, except that their offices were temporary, their salaries lower, and they also had charge over their own particular flocks.[15]

The Assembly which met at Perth in June 1563 granted such a commission to the Bishop of Caithness—Robert Stewart, brother of Matthew Earl of Lennox and uncle of Darnley (who, though apparently never consecrated, yet held the episcopal title)—to 'plant kirks' within his own bounds; in addition, three special Commissioners were then appointed for the North. John Hepburn, minister of Brechin, was to provide for churches in Moray, Banff, and the countries adjacent; Robert Pont (whom we shall meet again) was to plant kirks in the Sheriffdom of Inverness and around; and Donald Monro was appointed to plant kirks within the bounds of Ross, and to assist the Bishop of Caithness in preaching the gospel and planting kirks. Since there was yet no body such as the Presbytery which could exercise the functions of the old episcopal courts, these Superintendents and Commissioners were important figures in the new order; they watched over the work and life of the parochial clergy, and had power to suspend, deprive or transplant them; and they were 'to

[15] Calderwood, ii 183, 206, 224-5. Wodrow *Misc.*, i 322. Donaldson, 352-3, 359. Craven, 9-10.

procure the eradication of all monuments of idolatrie in the provinces or bounds assigned to them '.[16]

Monro, whose commission began at Lammas 1563, with the unusually high salary of 400 merks (just over £266), was the only Highlander among the three new Commissioners. A keen and critical eye was kept by the Church of John Knox even on those appointed to the highest office, and they were continually being reminded sharply of their duties and responsibilities. When the Assembly met at Edinburgh in December, it was complained of Monro that ' he was not so apt to teache as his charge required '; he attended in person, but was directed to withdraw while the complaint was being considered. Seven of the brethren were appointed ' to take a tryell of his gift, and to report to the Assemblie ', among them being John Erskine of Dun, Superintendent of Angus, and Robert Pont, now Commissioner of Moray. Their report has not survived among the records of the period, but we may infer that the outcome was favourable—or at least that the young Church could not afford to dispense with his services—from the fact that, when Monro's first commission expired, the Assembly of June 1564 continued it for another year. In practice, although the office was not held to be permanent, the same persons were usually reappointed; the duties were so arduous that ' ministers hunted not in these times for the offices of Superintendents and Commissioners ', and Monro's tenure in Ross spanned some twelve years. It is interesting to note that the old Collegiate Church of Tain, of which his uncle had been Provost, came into use for the Reformed worship, suffering little or none of the damage and decay (in its fabric at least) which at that time overtook so many

[16] Calderwood, ii 224-5. *Universall Kirk*, i 34. No contemporary evidence has been found to prove that the Commissioner was the same person as the former Archdeacon of the Isles, but the family genealogists are unanimous on the point, and Monro's connection with Buchanan (see pp. 26-7) makes it probable. The earliest authorities in which I find both appointments applied to the same person are the 18th-century Allan MS. and *Chron. Acc.*

ecclesiastical buildings. To it the Regent Moray presented a handsome pulpit—later stripped of most of its carvings, when the church was abandoned during the first half of the eighteenth century—which is a reminder that 'the good Regent' regarded the Reformers in that district as worthy of special honour or encouragement.[17]

But old customs die hard, and the Church in Ross was not without its troubles. At the Assembly of June 1565, held at Edinburgh, we find Monro complaining of the non-residence of two of his ministers—John Robertson of Urquhart (Treasurer of Ross) and John Watson of Alness. They were both ordered to return to their parishes under pain of disobedience to the Kirk. Ironically enough, five years later, when Monro reappears as Commissioner and Visitor-General, the same minister of Urquhart was appointed by the Assembly to assist him in his duties, 'because the said Commissioner was not prompt in the Scottish tongue'. This must have referred to his shortcomings in Gaelic, for in the district assigned to Monro that language (and not what we now know as Scots) was spoken, while the *Description* itself is evidence that he must have been familiar with the Lowland speech. Other Commissioners in the North suffered from the same disability, and Robert Pont had already found that he could do little in Moray 'for want of the Irish tongue'.[18]

There is no mention of Monro in the surviving records of the Assemblies held in the troubled years between 1565 and 1570. John Leslie, a staunch supporter of Queen Mary and the Roman Church, was now made Bishop of Ross. The Queen was forced to abdicate the throne after her defeat at Carberry Hill in June 1567, and following the escape from Lochleven a year later her cause suffered final

[17] *Reg. of Min.*, 51. Calderwood, ii 245, 282, iii 7. *Universall Kirk*, i 40, 51. Wodrow's *Collections*, 146. Wodrow *Misc.*, i 322. Knox, ii 292. *New Stat. Acc.*, xiv 290. Kennedy, 4.

[18] *Universall Kirk*, i 40, 63, 175. *Foulis Writs*, 24 (84). Calderwood, ii 244. Brown, 236 note.

eclipse at Langside. Bishop Leslie joined her in England, being deprived of his ecclesiastical revenues in his absence from the diocese. Meanwhile Huntly—the Lord Gordon of the 1553 bond—had been acting independently for Mary in the North, granting commissions in her name, until he surrendered to the young King's government in April 1569. That Munro also may have been a 'Queen's man' is suggested by a statement drawn up for Moray of the Queen's party's offences, dated 4th October 1568, in which 'Mr Donald Monroo "archden" of Ros an outlawed rebel' is mentioned as having been appointed by Huntly as Chamberlain to draw the rents of the Earldom of Ross.[19]

If Monro had indeed joined in the rising, he was back in the fold again by 1570. He was among the Superintendents and Commissioners appointed by the March Assemblies of 1572 and 1573 to meet the Lords of the Exchequer and to audit the accounts of the collectors of the thirds of the benefices, which could not be closed during the preceding years. 'For certain causes moving them', the 1573 Assembly also continued Monro for another term of office as Commissioner of Ross. At the August sitting, he was one of those appointed to confer on behalf of the Assembly with the Regent Morton and the Secret Council, to discuss the new Regent's proposals for the Church. Apparently for the last time, he was again continued as Commissioner until the Assembly to be held in March 1574. In the register of ministers and readers for that year he figures both as Commissioner and as minister of Lemlair, Kiltearn and Alness. Farquhar Monro was then reader at Kiltearn, and Alexander Morison at Alness, but the readership of Lemlair was vacant. Monro's annual stipend as minister was £66, 13s. 4d. Scots 'and the kirk lands', and

[19] *State Papers*, ii 516. For Leslie, see *D.N.B.*, xi 975-7. For Huntly, see Tytler, iii 309. Monro's old Bishop, Gordon, joined the Queen's party, but continued to exercise his ministerial functions (Donaldson, 357).

for supervising the eight other ministers and twenty-four readers in Ross he received £266, 13s. 4d.[20]

Donald Monro's name now disappears from the contemporary records. With the emergence of the violently anti-episcopal movement led by Andrew Melville, and the insistence on parity among the clergy, criticism of the long continuance of Commissioners in their offices was heard at the Assembly of August 1575. Some of the brethren feared that it would breed ' ambition and inconveniences ', and suggested that, where able men might be had, they should be changed from one district to another year by year. Several transfers were effected, but there is no report of any appointment for Ross, nor of any office being given to Monro. His name does not figure in a list of ministers for 1576, and new names appear against the charges of Kiltearn, Alness and Lemlair. It is supposed that Monro died about this time; he was unmarried, and was buried at Kiltearn, a little to the east of the burial ground of the family of Foulis. No stone marks his grave, and Donald Monro's only monument today is the little book bearing his name, which he himself never saw in print.[21]

[20] Calderwood, iii 275. *Universall Kirk*, i 257, 263-4, 281-2. *Thirds*, pp. xxxiii, 208. ' The Register of Ministers and Readers in the Kirk of Scotland, from the Book of the Assignation of Stipends, MDLXXIV ', in Wodrow *Misc.*, i 334-6.

[21] Calderwood, iii 253-4. Allan MS. Noble, 76. Robert Graham, Archdeacon of Ross in 1574, is referred to as Commissioner of Ross in March 1574, but he was appointed joint Commissioner of Caithness and Sutherland, and ' has no commission for Ross ' in 1575 (*Universall Kirk*, i 311, 321, 333). In ' The Buik of Assignationis ' for 1576 (MS. in Register House, extracts only published in *Reg. of Min.*, 71-97) there is no mention of Donald Monro ; Robert Monro appears as minister of Urquhart, Logy Wester, Kilterne and Alnes, and Donald Adamson as minister of Dingwell, Limlair, Urray and Contane. John Sandilands was parson of Kiltearn on 11 Aug. 1576 (*Foulis Writs*, 28 (90)).

3. THE BOOK

Among the outstanding men who sat with Monro in the early General Assemblies was George Buchanan, a notable figure in the councils of the Reformers, who was classical tutor to the young Queen and a Latin poet and scholar of European reputation. He was then collecting materials for his last and most ambitious work, *Rerum Scoticarum Historia*, for which he took pains to secure authentic accounts even of the remoter parts of the kingdom.

It was the fashion in those days, as it sometimes is still, for historians to set the stage for their narrative with a verbal description of the country whose story they are to tell. Buchanan found the early accounts of the Western Isles, in particular, to be full of fable and confusion, and decided to rely on later and surer authority. Fordun may have visited them in search of information two centuries before, but Buchanan's more recent predecessors—John Major, Hector Boece, and Bishop Leslie—seem to speak of the islands only from hearsay. Their outline was just beginning to take shape in the manuscript maps of the first half of the sixteenth century; the first satisfactory representation of the Western Isles in a printed map was in Mercator's map of the British Isles published at Duisburg in 1564, and this formed the basis of Ortelius' map of Scotland in his Atlas of 1573; but these maps seem to have been unknown to the Scottish historians of the period.[1]

Not until we come to the last of the great sixteenth century historians of Scotland do we find any evidence of his description of these Western Isles having been based on personal observation: not indeed on his own, for Buchanan was probably never in the Hebrides himself, but he clearly acknowledges his debt to one who knew them intimately. This was Donald Monro, whom he mentions as '*homo*

[1] *Fordun*, ii 386-8. Brown, 49 note. *Maps*, 10, 18, 21. Information from Dr A. B. Taylor. See also Mitchell, *List of Travels*.

doctus & pius', and '*hominem & pium, & diligentem, qui eas omne & ipse peragravit, & oculis perlustravit*'—a learned, godly and diligent man (as the first translator put it), 'who trauelled all these Iles vpon his feete, and saw them perfitly with his eyes'. Buchanan, who was a member of Assembly for four years before his election to the Moderator's chair in 1567, would know Monro and his record personally, and may well have had a part in his appointment as Commissioner of Ross. In his hands, Monro's *Description* became a flowing piece of prose, dovetailed into a general account of the country and its people. It forms eleven chapters in the first book of Buchanan's history, published as a handsome folio at Edinburgh in 1582, and was apparently among the last portions which he wrote, or at least revised.[2]

Not an island, nor even the smallest rock, which Monro had thought worthy of mention, was omitted by Buchanan. Much of the wealth of detail in the original was discarded, but little or nothing was added from other sources. Such a full account of the Hebrides had not been published before, and, as the appearance of Buchanan's *History* was an event of European importance, it had a wide circulation. The result was that the gist of Monro's *Description* found its way back to the Highlands and Islands, as well as to a wider public both in this country and abroad. The bards and *seanachies* of Clan Donald knew and even criticised Buchanan's work, and it was known also to an 'indweller' in Lewis who wrote an early account of that island. The first edition in English does not seem to have appeared until 1690, but there is a translation of the geographical portion dated 1603. Seemingly issued to enlighten the English at the Union of the Crowns, it forms part of a little book called *Certayne Matters concerning the Realme of Scotland*; the editor was John Monipennie, who later abridged the description slightly—omitting the acknowledgment to

[2] Buchanan, lib. i cap. xxxiv-xliv. Buchanan (Monipennie 1603). Buchanan (Aikman), lib. i cap. lxviii. Man, 12.

Monro in the process—for his better-known *Scots Chronicles*, published in 1612. Full credit was awarded to Monro in a later translation from Buchanan, for in John Lewis's *History of Great Britain* the seventh book is headed in bold type: 'The Description of the *Britannical* Ilandes, according to *Cambden*, and *Donald Monro*'. Some doubts seem to have lingered about the completeness of his island catalogue, however, for as late as 1633 Charles I granted an 'isle lying without the whole known and inhabited isles of the kingdom of Scotland' to Archibald, later Marquess of Argyll, who actually sent an expedition out in search of it. But the pioneer work in map-making done by Timothy Pont (whose father we have already encountered) tallies closely in its own medium with Monro's; and Buchanan's summary was reprinted in Blaeu's Scottish Atlas of 1654, which incorporated the surveys made by the younger Pont some 45 years before.[3]

In reading Buchanan's flowing Latin periods, however, it is only fair to remember that he condensed or omitted altogether much of the raw material provided by Monro. This goes far to explain what Martin Martin, the Skyeman who wrote (about 1695) the first comprehensive book on the Western Isles, had to say of his predecessor:—'Buchanan had his information from Donald Monro, who had been in many of them; and therefore his account is the best that has hitherto appeared, but it must be owned that it is very imperfect; that great man designed the history, and not the geography of his country, and therefore in him it was pardonable. Besides since his time there is a great change in the humour of the world, and by consequence in the way of

[3] 'The Book of Clanranald' in *Rel. Celt.*, ii 170-1. 'History of the Macdonalds' in *H.P.*, i 10-11. Description of Lewis by 'John Morisone, indweller there' in *Spot. Misc.*, ii 338, and Macfarlane, ii, pp. xxiv, 211. J. Maitland Anderson, *The Writings and Portraits of George Buchanan* (1906), 19. Buchanan (Monipennie, 1612), in *Misc. Scot.*, i 175-88. Lewis, 227-43. *Hist. MSS.*, iv 482. John Willcock, *The Great Marquess* (1903), 24, 25. Writs of the 'Unfound Isle' (Argyle Inventory) quoted in *O.P.S.*, ii (i) 380. Blaeu, 136-50.

writing. Natural and experimental philosophy has been much improved since his days; and therefore descriptions of countries, without the natural history of them, are now justly reckoned to be defective '.[4]

But although most writers, like Martin, were content to accept Monro's *Description* at second hand, the existence of a fuller version was known to some. What became of the original is not known, although one copy was ' said to be done from his Papers '. The earliest copy now extant—and it is incomplete—was made in 1642 by Sir James Balfour of Denmilne and Kinnaird, a Fife laird who was Lyon King of Arms to Charles I, and one of the first Scotsmen to realise the value of original documents in the study of history; comparison of his transcript with Buchanan shows that three considerable groups of islands have been omitted—including part of Monro's account of Islay and Lismore, and the whole of Tiree and Coll, and Bernera (Harris)—either by a defect in the original, or by careless copying. Balfour's manuscripts eventually found their way into the Advocates' Library in Edinburgh (now the National Library of Scotland), where they are now the property of the nation. The next transcript—that on which the present edition is based—appears to have been made some forty years later under the supervision of Sir Robert Sibbald, Charles II's physician and his Geographer for Scotland, who collected a vast amount of material for a natural history and geographical description of the country. William Nicolson, in his *Scottish Historical Library* published while he was Archdeacon of Carlisle in 1702, mentions Monro's *Description* as being then ' still in manuscript ', and in 1733 Sibbald's copy also was acquired by the Advocates' Library. A third manuscript, made about 1749 by Walter Macfarlane of that Ilk, the antiquary and genealogist, has the same omissions as Balfour's, of which it may have been a copy. In each of these three collections, a transcript of the

[4] Martin, 61.

Genealogies appears along with the *Description*; it has been suggested that the account of the manners of the Highlanders and Islanders, with which Buchanan prefaced his summary of Monro, was also borrowed from him, but if so no manuscript has been found to prove it.[5]

So far, then, Monro's *Description* was known to comparatively few, and it was not until some 200 years after his death that it entered upon a new phase. It appeared as the leading item in a small volume of tracts about the Hebrides, published by William Auld at Edinburgh in 1774, and now very scarce. With it were printed the *Genealogies*, supplemented by some 'Observations upon Surnames' by the first Earl of Marchmont; a brief 'Account of Hirta and Rona' by Sir George Mackenzie of Tarbat, given to Sir Robert Sibbald in 1680 and published for the first time; and two other works on St Kilda which had already been printed, by the Rev. Alexander Buchan and Martin Martin. All the sub-titles bear the date 1773, but they do not seem to have been published separately. Who prepared the little volume for press is not known, but in spite of imperfections it has proved the model for all but one of the later editions until now. There is neither preface nor introduction, but an 'Advertisement' states that, if the tracts meet with a favourable reception, 'several originals of the same kind will be presented by the Publisher'; and he does not seem to have been disappointed, for in the following year he reprinted two genealogical works by William Buchanan of Auchmar, of which we shall hear again presently. This first edition of Monro contains one or two errors, which have been perpetuated and added to by later editors; but the worst fault is its incompleteness. Richard Gough, in his *British Topography* published only six years later, says

[5] See note on 'The Manuscripts' (pp. 148-50). Mackie, esp. 7, 19. Autobiography of Sir R. Sibbald in *Analecta*, i 142. Nicolson (1702), 55. Buchanan's preface (pp. 41-4) is attributed to Monro by Lewis (p. 234) and by a writer in *The Scotsman*, 28 Feb. 1881; and by Rev. A. C. Sutherland in *Transactions of the Gaelic Society of Inverness* (1878), vii 6.

that Auld used a manuscript in the Advocates' Library, which was ' the best and correctest copy '.[6]

The Hebrides were now becoming known to the outside world, and the little book soon attracted attention. The Welsh naturalist and traveller, Thomas Pennant, who visited the islands in 1772, must have obtained a copy after his return home; for in his *Voyage to the Hebrides*, published two years later, he refers his readers to its pages, and says, in writing of Iona:—' I was very desirous of viewing the tombs of the Kings, described by the DEAN of the isles, and from him by Buchanan '. To Dr Johnson, who came to Scotland with Boswell in 1773, Monro would be known (if at all) only through the pages of the great historian; perhaps the Doctor, an admirer of Buchanan's writings, would have been less enthusiastic about Monro's rugged phrases, for even of the more polished Martin he once said: ' A man could not write so ill, if he should try '. Boswell probably knew Buchanan's account of the Hebrides, but he wrongly attributes to him the Latinisation *Insula Porcorum* for the Isle of Muck (which is actually from Fordun), instead of *Porcaria*. Another writer who borrowed from Monro through Buchanan was William Collins, whose ' Ode on the Popular Superstitions of the Highlands of Scotland ' mentions the chapel ' in whose small vaults a pigmy-folk are found '.[7]

A second edition of the *Description* and *Genealogies*—the first entirely devoted to Monro's work—followed in 1805. It is a slim little volume of 40 pages, printed in Edinburgh

[6] Lowndes, iii 1283, and new edn. pt. vi 1585. Dr J. A. Smith in *P.S.A.S.*, xiv 439. Mitchell, 32. Gough, ii 732 note. Lord Marchmont's ' Observations ' were reprinted from Jeremy Collier, *The Great Historical, Geographical, Genealogical and Poetical Dictionary* (2nd edn., 1750), ii *s.v.* Surname. See note H : Errors in Earlier Editions (p. 136) ; it is clear that Auld did not use *Sib.* MS., but internal evidence leaves one in doubt whether he used *Bal.* or *Macf.*, or neither.

[7] Pennant, i 180, 215, 218, 225, 243, 256, 272, 275, 285, 292, 293, 295, 319, 322, 327, 331. Boswell's *Johnson*, 157, 205, 448, 597 ; *Journal*, 18 Sep. 1773. *Fordun*, i 43, ii 388. Collins' ' Ode ', though first published in 1788, is believed to have been written about 1749.

for Archibald Constable & Company by J. Stark, Toddrick's Wynd, High Street. One or two minor alterations in the text make their appearance, but this edition—which was used by Sir Walter Scott in writing *The Lord of the Isles*, as he acknowledged in the notes—also starts several errors which remained uncorrected by later editors.[8]

A flood of tourists, confined to Britain by Napoleon's blockade and urged northward by the magic pen of Scott, found their way to the Highlands and Islands during the early years of last century. There was a fresh demand for all that had been written on these regions, and both Monro's works were reprinted as part of the *Miscellanea Scotica*, introduced on its title-page as ' a Collection of Tracts relating to the History, Antiquities, Topography, and Literature of Scotland ' . The *Description* was given a place in the second volume, published at Glasgow in 1818; while—to the confusion of later writers, who failed to locate them—the *Genealogies* followed two years later in volume four, sandwiched awkwardly between the two works by Buchanan of Auchmar already mentioned. Once again Monro marched in company with Mackenzie, Buchan and Martin on St Kilda, and now he was joined also by his imitator, Monipennie, the pilot's instructions for King James's voyage round Scotland, and other suitable fellow-travellers. Further textual errors crept in, but the worst blemish in this edition, which has misled many later writers, is that the *Description* is dated ' 1594 ' on the title-page, instead of 1549.[9]

[8] Scott, canto i and note, canto iii and note, canto iv and note. See note H (p. 136).

[9] *Misc. Scot.*, ii 111-53, iv 121-4 ; Maidment is said to have been the editor by C. S. Terry (*The Rising of 1745, with a Bibliography of Jacobite History* (1900), 260), but it is not in T. G. Stevenson, *The Bibliography of James Maidment* (1883). Monro's *Description* (1884 edn.), 6. Mackie, 19 note. Monro's *Genealogies* were not included in previous editions of Auchmar's works (1723 and 1775). For ' 1594 ' error perpetuated see *e.g. Spot. Misc.*, ii 375 ; John Stuart, *Sculptured Stones of Scotland* (Spalding Club, 1867), ii 26 ; Reeves, 324 ; Muir (1885), 54, 273 ; Cumming, 88, 133 ; Stewart, 19 ; Neil M. Gunn, *Off in a Boat* (1938), 229. See note H (p. 136).

So far there had been little in the way of direct commentary on Monro's work, but it is appropriate at this point to discuss the most serious attack ever made on his reliability. It appears in a set of four volumes on the Highlands and Western Isles, written in the form of letters to Sir Walter Scott, and published in 1824. The author was Dr John MacCulloch, the geologist remembered as 'the Stone Doctor', who had made a series of annual journeys between 1811 and 1821. Rejoicing in the sport now known as 'debunking', he set down his conclusions on subjects ranging from the rocks to the bagpipes with a racy and caustic pen, and fell upon Donald Monro with vigour. He criticised his statement that '48 crownit Scottish kings' were buried in Iona; finding no reference in the *Description* to a certain ruined island chapel, he charged Monro with ignorance of his diocese; and, unable to identify most of the islands in Monro's list, accused him of using his imagination and imposing on his readers' credulity. But what are the facts? [10]

On the tombs in Iona, 'his authority is worth very little, though Buchanan has idly given it currency', says MacCulloch; 'the Dean's kings may have been Highland chiefs: or it is as likely that they were some of the gentlemen who, on the same authority [*i.e.* Buchanan's], are buried in Iona and are now flourishing in the gallery of Holyrood House'. Whether in fact these 48 kings ever reigned, or were buried in Iona, may, as MacCulloch implies, be open to question; but to cast doubt on Monro's authority on this ground would only be justified if Monro had vouched for the story himself. Actually Monro says that it is related by old Scottish and Irish chroniclers; that is an interesting tradition, and worth recording, and so he recorded it—a very different thing from stating it as a fact. In this instance Monro says

[10] MacCulloch (1824), ii 89, iii 144, 274, iv 162-5. Criticisms also in *Trans. Inverness Scientific Society and Field Club*, ix 171 ; Nicolson (1930), 97, 431 ; Donald Buchanan, *Reflections on the Isle of Barra* (1942), 59-60.

too much, but elsewhere he says too little to please MacCulloch, who complains that Monro had passed the ruins on Inch Cormac without notice—'as he has done nearly everything else for which, from the nature of his office, we should especially look to him for information. If he had been Verger instead of Dean, he could not have been much more ignorant of the diocese to which he belonged'. We have seen on what grounds Monro's accuracy in matters of fact has been impugned: now he is attacked for omitting that on which he as a clergyman should have been fully informed. MacCulloch does not trouble to enquire the purpose for which Monro's *Description* was compiled; and that it was not merely to satisfy the curious (like his own) may at least be affirmed with confidence. No work of description can be all-embracing, and to assume, because a subject is not discussed, that the author must have been ignorant of it is merely showing a wish to criticise. On this we may borrow Dr Johnson's words in defence of Pennant: 'He has not said what he has to tell, so you cannot find fault with him for what he has not told'.[11]

Again, MacCulloch blames 'the older writers' for carelessness in giving the place-names of the Western Isles; this fault, he says, 'will be very evident in looking into Monro's book, in which it is scarcely possible to recognise one in ten of them'. And later he says, of the Pigmies' Isle in Lewis, that there was no such island as Monro described, unless it was one of the Flannan group; 'we have no recourse [declared MacCulloch] but to think that he has been either dreaming, or trying experiments on his readers. It is, perhaps, well that his book is so little and so vacant; if the rest of what is meant for truth is like this specimen, the less of it the better'. Place-names, as

[11] 'We know more of the general appearance of these islands at the period with which we are dealing than of any other part of the kingdom,' on the authority of Monro (P. Hume Brown, *Scotland in the Time of Queen Mary* (1904), 29). Boswell's *Journal*, 17 Sep. 1773.

MacCulloch himself admits, are often altered in transmission, and even some of those in his own books are now unknown—two of them being the very same as those given by Monro. John F. Campbell of Islay thought 'the names of the islands and families, as now pronounced, could hardly be better expressed for English ears'. Professor Hume Brown was able to identify 121 out of the 209 islands in the printed version of Monro which MacCulloch knew; and the present editor has located 224 out of a total of 251 with reasonable certainty, both on the current Ordnance Survey maps and in the *West Coast Pilot.* It is doing Monro less than justice to suppose that the remainder existed only in his imagination. Blaeu's maps, which were in print long before MacCulloch's day, form the best guide to Monro's list; a glance at them, or at John Adair's map of Scotland in the later editions of Buchanan's *History*, shows at once the position of the Pigmies' Isle, which has been rediscovered in our own day by that very method.[12]

In short, MacCulloch's gibes can be dismissed as the result of careless first impressions, or of an unjustified prejudice against Monro. Although so poorly founded, however, they were 'idly given currency' in a guide to the Highlands and Islands so late as 1877; but nothing shows more clearly that Monro's *Description* has survived them unscathed than the fact that it has been reprinted four times since MacCulloch wrote. The next edition—the last to be confined to his work alone, until the present—appeared in 1884, when the land agitation and the work of the Napier Crofters Commission had led to a revival of public interest in the Highlands and Islands. Limited to 250 copies, it was published by Thomas D. Morison, Glasgow, and printed at the University Press by Robert MacLehose, uniform with Martin's later and fuller book, reissued by

[12] J. F. Campbell, *Popular Tales of the West Highlands* (1862), iv 357. MacCulloch knew Pont's maps and Blaeu (iii 141). For changes in names see Appendix II (pp. 112-3), and for the Pigmies Isle see note F (p. 133).

them in the same year. The editing leaves something to be desired, and there is evidence that the text is founded upon the 1818 edition, even to the extent of repeating obvious errors in numbering. It is nowhere mentioned that the *Description* forms the basis of that given by Buchanan; the title-page of the 1774 edition is incorrectly quoted; and it is stated that the *Genealogies* were not included in the *Miscellanea Scotica*.[13]

In each of its next three appearances, Monro's work forms part of a larger collection. For the first time, however, it was submitted to a critical examination by a professional historian, when Hume Brown included the full text (as then known) of the *Description* in his *Scotland before 1700, from Contemporary Documents*, published in 1893. Here it was usefully set alongside the work of earlier writers such as Fordun and Boece, and the first attempt was made to identify the islands enumerated by Monro. It is surprising that, with all his attention to detail, Hume Brown did not check his text with Buchanan's; had he done so, he would at once have realised its incompleteness, and might have set about trying to fill the gaps. As it was, he collated the two manuscripts known to him, following each according as it seemed to present the better reading. But this did not prevent him from carrying into his text several of the first editor's mistakes; one of these—'fostering of thieves, ruggairs, and reivars, till a nail, upon the peilling and spulzeing of poure people', as it was copied—he ingeniously explained by a footnote declaring 'the meaning is that they carried off everything *even to a nail*'; had he looked more closely at his manuscripts, he would have found that 'till a nail' is a misreading for 'till await'. Nevertheless, this edition had the effect of placing the study of Monro's

[13] Miller's *Royal Tourist Handbook to the Highlands and Islands* (edn. *c.* 1877), 350-1; MacCulloch is quoted by name at p. 21. It has been stated that Martin's book (and so perhaps Monro's also?) was reprinted for the use of the Napier Commission (William Mackenzie, *Skye: Iochdar-Trotternish* (1930), 124), but I have been unable to confirm.

work on a surer footing, and no one who follows can afford to ignore Hume Brown's comments. Incidentally, this is the only edition in which Monro's *Description* has been printed without the *Genealogies*, which were not appropriate to the historian's purpose. A new text of both works, based on the manuscripts of Walter Macfarlane of that Ilk, appeared in the third volume of Macfarlane's *Geographical Collections*, edited for the Scottish History Society by Sir Arthur Mitchell and Mr J. T. Clark, and published in 1908. Finally, Monro's *Description* and *Genealogies* were added to 'round off' a new edition of Martin's *Description of the Western Islands of Scotland*, published by Eneas Mackay of Stirling in 1934. There are no notes or commentary, but one or two minor features of the earliest edition have been restored, and several misreadings corrected. Although still marred by a few errors, this might well have remained the standard text but for that now made available in the present work.[14]

Extracts from Monro's *Description* and (to a lesser extent) his *Genealogies* have appeared in many topographical and historical works, and he is one of the most frequently quoted authorities on the Western Isles. None would now disagree with Hume Brown's statement that Monro's little book is interesting at once to the antiquary, the geographer and the philologist, and that, though the description founded upon it by Buchanan is the more flowing narrative, the original, by the minuteness of its detail and the language in which it is written, has a far higher historical value.[15]

[14] Brown, 236-72. Macfarlane, iii 260-302. Martin, 477-526.
[15] *Islay* (1895), 475-7. Campbell, 31-6. Stewart, 65-7. Brown, 237.

MONRO'S
WESTERN ISLES
with
Buchanan's Preface

PREFACE TO MONRO'S DESCRIPTION

BY

George Buchanan

This extract from his *Rerum Scoticarum Historia* (1582) immediately precedes Buchanan's description of the Western Islands, which was based chiefly on Donald Monro. The translation is that of James Aikman.

It now remains that I say something concerning the islands, that part of the British history which is involved in the greatest confusion. Setting aside, therefore, the more ancient writers, from whom it is impossible to extract any information, I shall follow the writers of our own time, upon whose accuracy and veracity more reliance may be placed.

The islands which as it were surround Scotland form three distinct classes, the Western, the Orcades, and the Zetland isles. Those are called the Western isles which are spread over the Deucaledonian sea, on the west side of Scotland, from Ireland almost to the Orcades. The British historians, of the last and the present age, commonly style them the Hebrides, certainly a new name, of whose origin no trace can be found among ancient writers. In that part of the ocean some place the Æbudæ, or Æmodæ; but they are at so much variance among themselves, that they scarcely ever agree in situation, number, or name.

Strabo, to begin with the oldest, may perhaps be excused for having followed uncertain report, that part of the world not having then been sufficiently explored. Mela enumerates seven Hemodæ, Martianus Capella as many Acmodæ, Ptolemy and Solinus five Æbudæ, and Pliny seven Acmodæ, and thirty Æbudæ. I shall retain the name most frequently used by the ancients, and designate the whole of the Western Islands Æbudæ. Their site, relative condition, and produce,

I shall describe from more recent and more certain authority; following chiefly Donald Monro, a pious and diligent man, who went over the whole of them himself, and minutely inspected them in person.

They lie scattered in the Deucaledonian sea, upwards of three hundred in number, and from time immemorial belonged to the kings of the Scots, until the time of Donald, the brother of Malcolm the third, who ceded them to the king of Norway, in order to obtain his assistance in his unjust usurpation of the Scottish crown. The Danes and Norwegians retained them for about one hundred and sixty years, until being vanquished in a decisive battle by Alexander the third, of Scotland, they restored them. Sometimes, however, trusting to their strength, and enticed into seditions, the islanders have asserted their liberty, and erected kings of their own. Among others, John, of the family of Donald, lately usurped the royal title.

In their food, clothing, and in the whole of their domestic economy, they adhere to ancient parsimony. Hunting and fishing, supply them with food. They boil the flesh with water poured into the paunch or the skin of the animal they kill, and in hunting sometimes they eat the flesh raw, merely squeezing out the blood. They drink the juice of the boiled flesh. At their feasts they sometimes use whey, after it has been kept for several years, and even drink it greedily; that species of liquor they call bland, but the greater part quench their thirst with water. They make a kind of bread, not unpleasant to the taste, of oats and barley, the only grain cultivated in these regions, and, from long practice, they have attained considerable skill in moulding the cakes. Of this they eat a little in the morning, and then contentedly go out a hunting, or engage in some other occupation, frequently remaining without any other food till the evening.

They delight in variegated garments, especially stripped, and their favourite colours are purple and blue. Their ancestors wore plaids of many different colours, and numbers still retain this custom, but the majority, now, in their dress, prefer a dark brown, imitating nearly the leaves of the heather, that when lying upon the heath in the day, they may not be discovered by the appearance of their clothes; in these, wrapped rather than covered, they brave the severest storms in the open air, and sometimes lay themselves down to sleep even in the midst of snow.

In their houses, also, they lie upon the ground; strewing fern, or heath, on the floor, with the roots downward and the leaves turned up. In this manner they form a bed so pleasant, that it may vie in softness with the finest down, while in salubrity it far exceeds it; for heath, naturally possessing the power of absorption, drinks up the superfluous moisture, and restores strength to the fatigued nerves, so that those who lie down languid and weary in the evening, arise in the morning vigorous and sprightly. They have all, not only the greatest contempt for pillows, or blankets, but, in general, an affectation of uncultivated roughness and hardihood, so that when choice, or necessity induces them to travel in other countries, they throw aside the pillows, and blankets of their hosts, and wrapping themselves round with their own plaids, thus go to sleep, afraid lest these barbarian luxuries, as they term them, should contaminate their native simple hardiness.

Their defensive armour consists of an iron headpiece, and a coat of mail, formed of small iron rings, and frequently reaching to the heels. Their weapons are, for the most part, a bow, and arrows barbed with iron, which cannot be extracted without widely enlarging the orifice of the wound; but a few carry swords or Lochaber axes. Instead of a trumpet, they use a bagpipe. They are exceedingly fond of music, and employ harps of a peculiar kind, some of which are strung with brass, and some with catgut. In playing they strike the wires either with a quill, or with their nails, suffered to grow long for the purpose; but their granp ambition is to adorn their harps with great quantities of silver and gems, those who are too poor to afford jewels substituting crystals in their stead. Their songs are not inelegant, and, in general, celebrate the praises of brave men; their bards seldom choosing any other subject. They speak the ancient Gaelic language a little altered.

NOTE ON THE TEXT

S refers to Sibbald MS. of Monro
B refers to Balfour MS. of Monro
M refers to Macfarlane MS. of Monro
Buch. refers to Buchanan's *Historia*

Details of these are given under PRINCIPAL SOURCES on pp.148-51

The basic text is that of *S*. Footnotes are confined to textual matters, and commentary will be found in the Introduction, Appendices, Notes and Glossary. The present forms of all the islands identified, as they appear in the *West Coast Pilot* or the one-inch Ordnance Survey maps, as well as Monro's spellings, are given in the Index.

Variant readings in *B* and *M*, where they amplify *S*, differ essentially from it, or appear to clarify the meaning—but not where they simply involve minor variations in spelling—are given in the footnotes, with occasional references to *Buch.* I have endeavoured to present the original reading of *S*, but the text is sometimes made difficult by later interlineations and amendments. Usually these merely alter place-names to the spelling in *B*, and they are ignored in all but exceptional cases ; where given they are indicated by the abbreviation *sec. manu.*

Words and phrases printed within [square brackets] are not in *S*, and have been supplied from *B* and *M*.

There is nothing to show that Monro gave any numbers to the islands in his list ; I have therefore adopted my own numbering, slightly different from that in *S*. To make comparison easier, numbers given in the previous editions—taken from *B* and *M*—are added in *italics*.

The textual reasons for preferring *S* to the other two MSS. may be summarised as follows :

a) it includes three groups, totalling 43 islands [Nos. 54-69, 110-120, 187-202], three connecting paragraphs [between Nos. 15/16, 225/226, and 248/249], and fuller accounts of two other islands [Nos. 53 and 70], all omitted in *B* and *M*, but given in *Buch.* ;

b) it places Nos. 203-224 in the same order as *Buch.*, instead of between Nos. 248/249, as in *B* and *M* ;

c) in several details where it differs from *B* and *M*, the reading is more closely akin to *Buch.* [see footnotes to Nos. 53, 126, 145-49 and 186], or more accurate [Nos. 91, 182] ;

d) some island names are nearer to the form given in *Buch.* and those in use today than in *B* and *M* [Nos. 126, 143, 182, 231].

On the other hand, there are some details in which *S* compares unfavourably with *B* and *M* [see *e.g.* footnotes to Nos. 70, 136, 226], and some passages in *Buch.* which are omitted in *S* as well as in *B* and *M* [Nos. 2, 3, 37, 164, 249].

DESCRIPTION OF THE OCCIDENTAL *i.e.* WESTERN ISLES OF SCOTLAND

BY

MR DONALD MONRO

who travelled through many of them in Anno. 1549

[1. *1.*] First in the Ireland-seas foregainst the points of Galloway, mid-sea nearest betwixt England, Ireland and Scotland lyes the first Isle of the foresaid Isles called in the Latine tongue Mona, sive Sodora, in English *Man*, and in Irish leid called Maniun;[1] quhilk sometime (as auld auncient Historiographers shaws) was wont to be the seat first ordained by Finnan king of Scots to the Priests and Philosophers called in Latin Druides or Driudes; in English Culdees, or Worshippers of God; and in Irish leid Draiche,[2] quhilks were the first teachers of Religion in Albion. Whereinto is the Cathedral Kirk of the Bishoprey of Man and Isles dedicat in the honour of Peter Apostle. The Isle is 24 mile lang and 8 mile braid, with 2 Castles in it.

[2. *2.*] Northwart fra this Isle of Man 60 miles of sea lyes *Ellsay* an Isle of ane mile lang, quhairin is ane great heich hill round and roche, and als abundant of Solan-geese,[3] and ane small point of ane Ness quhairat the Fisher-boats lyes: for the same Isle is very good for fishing, sic as Keiling,

Title. 'Description of the Occidental *i.e.* Western Isles of Scotland' rewritten over original by another hand, and probably at the same time 'by Mr Donald Monro who travelled through many of them in Anno 1549' added. In *B* and *M* the title-page reads: 'A Descriptione of the Westerne Iles of Scotland called Hybrides. Compiled By Mr Donald Monro, Deane of the Iles. 1549'.

[1] Manain *BM*. (see explanation of contractions at p. 44.

[2] Overwritten, as in *BM*.

[3] *Buch.* (fol. 9) says: frequens est *cuniculis*, auibusque marinis (it abounds with Conies and Sea-Fowls—1690 trans.).

Ling and other white fishes. Forenent this Isle lyes Carrick on the south-east part, Ireland on the south-west part, and the Lands of Kintyre on the west and north-west part; the said Ellsay being marchand midsea betwixt the said Marches.

[3. *3*.] Benorth or north-east fra this Isle 24 miles of sea lyes *Aran* a great Isle full of great mountains and forrests good for hunting, with part of woods; extending in length fra the Kyle of Aran to Castle-Donan southwart to 24 mile, and fra Drum donin to the West Kilbreid 16 mile braid, inhabite only at the sea-coasts. Herein are 3 Castles: ane callit Braizay pertaining to the Earle of Aran; ane other auld house called the Castle of heid of Loch Ranesay pertaining to the said Earle; and the third called Castle Donan pertaining first to ane of the Stewarts of Buit his bluid called Mr James, quha and his bluid are the best men in the countrey. In Aran is an Loch callit Loch-Renasay with three or four small Lochis [4] and twa paroch-kirks, the ane callit Kilbreid, the other called Kilmure. Forenent this Isle lyes the coast of Kyle in the east and south-west be 10 or 12 [5] mile of sea, in the north Buit be 8 mile of sea, in the west Scibbenes pertaining to my Lord of Argile.[6]
[4. *4*.] Upon the shore of the Isle lyes *Flada* ane little Isle full of Conyngis with ane other Isle called the Isle of

[4] waters *BM.*

[5] 16 or 18 *sec. manu.*

[6] the Earle of Ergyle *BM. Buch.* (fol. 9) adds : Mare qua humilior est, irrumpens in ea sinum satis magnum facit : cuius aditum claudit insula Molas. Itaque montibus vndique se attollentibus, ac ventorum impetum frangentibus portus nauibus intus est tutissimus : & in aquis perpetuo tranquillis piscatio adeo copiosa, vt si quid ultra, quam quod in vnum diem sit satis capiatur, accolæ in mare, tanquam in piscinam id projiciant. (Where it [the ground] is lowest the sea forms a pretty large bay, whose entrance is protected by the island Molas, besides which, the mountains towering on every side break the force of the wind, and render it a very safe harbour for shipping. In these waters, perpetually tranquil, the fishing is so abundant, that if more be caught than what are required, for one day, the inhabitants throw them back again into the sea, as into a fish pond—Aikman's trans.).

[5. *5.*] *Molass* quherein there was foundit be John of the Isles [7] ane Monasterie of Friers which is decayed.

[6. *6.*] The Isle of *Buit* lyes (as we have said before [8] 8 miles of sea to the northeast fra this Isle of Aran ane mane Isle 8 mile lang fra the north to the south, and 4 mile braid fra the west to the east, very fertile ground, namely for aits with twa strengths. The ane is the Round Castle of Buit callit Revsay [9] of the auld; and about it ane Burrowstoun callit Buitt. Before the Town and the Castle is ane Kay [10] of the sea, quhilk is an gude heavin for schippis to ly on ankeris. That other Castle is callit the Castle of Kames, quhilk Kames in Irish is alsmekle to say as ane Bay in English: for under it is ane Bay of the sea, and sa should it be callit in English the Bay Castle. In this yle thair is twa paroche-kirks of that ane south callit the Kirk of Breid; [11] the uther north in the Burrowstoun of Buitt callit Kilbrink, with twa chapellis, ane of thame above the toun of Buit, and the uther under the forsaid Castle of Kames. On the north and north-west of this Ile be ane half mile of sea lyes the coast of Argile, the east side of it the coast of Cunyngham, be 6 myle of sea. On the west south-west of this Ile
[7. *7.*] foirsaid lyes ane little Ile callit *Inismerog* twa myle of sea law main ground well inhabite and manurit, ane myle lang, half myle braid.

[8. *8.*] On the east and south-east of this Ile lyes ane Ile callit *Cumbray* inhabite and manurit, 3 myle lang, ane myle braid, with ane Kirk callit St Colms Kirk.

[9. *9.*] Besides this Ile of Cumbray lyes ane uther Ile callit *Cumbray of the Dais* because there is mony Dais in it.[12]

[7] Johne Lord of the Iles *BM.*

[8] Bracket unclosed.

[9] ? Rersay ; Rothesay *sec. manu* ; Rosaia *Buch.* ; Rosay *BM.*

[10] Bay *BM.*

[11] Bryde *B*, Bride *M.*

[12] It hath 2 houses on a little island with which at low water thair is communication *sec. manu.*

[10. *10.*] Before the south point of the Promonterie of Kintyre lyis be ane lang myle of sea ane Ile neirest ane myle lang callit the Ile of *Avoin*, quhilk Ile has obteinit that name fra the Armes of Denmark, quhilk Armes are callit in thair leid Havoin, inhabite and manurit, gude for schippis to ly on ankeris. Foranent this Ile on the schoir of Kintyre [*11.*] lyes a stark Castell sumtime callit Carrik-steach with ane little water, wherein there is ane gude heavin for small boats, and this Avoin is ane common place for schippis.

[11. *12.*] On the south-west fra the Promonterie of Kintyre upon the coast of Irland be 4 myle to the land lyis an Ile callit *Rachlind* perteining to Irland and possest thir many zeiris by Clandonald of Kintyre, 4 myle lang, 2 myle braid, gude land inhabite and manurit.

[12. *13.*] Upon the north-west coast of Kintyre be 4 myle of the sea to the sun lyis ane little Ile callit *Caray* with ane chapell in it, gude for quhyte fisches, abundante of conyngis, inhabite and manurit, mair nor ane myle lang, half myle breid.

[13. *14.*] At the heid of this Ile lyand from this Ile in the north-east lyis ane Ile callit *Gighay* 6 myle lang, ane myle half mile breid with a Paroche-Kirk, gude fertile mane land, abundante of edderis in it. The auld Thane of Gighay sould be laird of the same callit M^c^neill of Gighay, and now is possest be the Clandonald streker at the schoir of Kintyre from the south-west to the north-east, in length four myle of sea from Kintyre.

[14. *15.*] Narrest that Ile layis *Diuray* ane uther fine forrest for deiris, inhabite and manurit at the coist side, part be Clandonald of Kintyre, part be M^c^gillane of Doward part be M^c^gillane of Loche of Boy, and part be M^c^dufifithe of Collinsay, ane Ile of 24 mile of lenth, lyand from the south-west to the north-eist 12 mile of sea from Gighay above-written, and ane myle from Ila quhairin thair is twa lochis meittand utheris throw the mid-ile of salt water to the lenth of half myle. And all the deiris of the west part of the forrest will be callit be tynchells to that narow entres, and the next day callit west again be tynchells throw the said narow entres, and infinit deir slain there.[13] Part of small woods in it. This Ile, as the Ancients alledges, sould be called Deray, taking the name from the deiris in norn leid, quhilk hes given it that name in auld tymes ago. In this Ile thair is twa gude Raidis and safety for schippis; the ane callit Lubnalenray,[14] the uther Lochcerbart.[15] Foiranent uther is the greatest hills thairin [are chieflie] Ben quheillis, Ben senta corben, Ben noir[16] in Ardlayfasay.[17] Ane chapell sumtyme the paroche kirk Kilernadill.[18] The watter of Laxay thair, the water of Udergane, the water of Glengargaster, the water of Knokbrek and ill caray avin villi.[19] All this wateris salmond slane on thame. This Ile is full of noble Cows[20] with certane fresche water Lochis nocht mekle of profeit.

[15. *16.*] Narrest this Ile be twa myle lyis ane Ile callit *Scarbay*. Betwixt thir 2 Ilis thair runs ane stream above the power of all sailing and rowing with infinite dangeris callit Arey brekan.[21] This stream is 8 myle lang, quhilk may not be hantit but be certane tydes. This Scarbay is 4 myle lang from the west to the eist, ane myle braid, ane heich Roche Ile inhabite and manurit with some woods in it.

Efter this Scarbay lyis mony small Ilis not mekle of profit, notwithstanding thot neidfull to write all thair names as after followis.[22]

[13] No new sentence in *BM*.
[14] Lubnaleirey *BM*.
[15] Loche Terbart *BM*.
[16] Ben cheilis, Bin senta, Corben, Ben an noyre *BM*.
[17] No new sentence in *BM*.
[18] Kiternadill *M*.
[19] Knockbraich, Lindill, Caray, Auanbilley *BM*.
[20] coillis *BM*.
[21] Corybrekkan *B*, Corybrekan *M*.
[22] This paragraph not in *BM*; Post hanc multæ ignobiles insulæ deinde sparguntur *Buch*. fol. 9.

[16. *17.*] Narrest this layis [ane iyle, callit in Erische] *Ellan wellich* in the north-eist.

[17. *18.*] Narrest this lyis ane [very] little Ile callit *Gewrastill.*

[18. *19.*] Narrest this Ile lyis ane little Ile callit *Lungay.*

[19. *20.*] Narrest this Ile lyis [ane iyle callit] *Fidlay chaillie.*

[20. *21.*] Narrest this Ile lyis ane little Ile callit [in Erische] *Fidlainrow.*

[21. *22.*] Narrest this Ile layis ane little Ile [in Erische] callit *Garvhelach skean.*

[22. *23.*] Narrest this Ile lyis ane little Ile[23] callit [in Erische] *Garvhelach na monaodh.*

[23. *24.*] Narrest this Ile lyis ane [verey] little Ile callit [in Erische] *Ellach nanaobh.*

[24. *25.*] Narrest this Ile lyis ane little Ile callit [in the Erische Leid] *Culbrenyn.*

[25. *26.*] Narrest thir foirsaids small Iles lyis ane Ile callit *Dunchonill* sa namet from Conill Kernoch ane strength, and alsmekle to say in English as ane round Castell.

[26. *27.*] Narrest this lyis ane Ile callit *Ellan a mhadi* [in Erische] callit in English the Wolfis Ile.

[27. *28.*] Narrest this layis [ane Iylland callit in Erische] *Belnachua* quhair thair is fair skailzie aneuch.

[28. *29.*] Narrest this lyis [the small Iyle of] *Ellan vickeran.*

[29. *30.*] Narrest this lyis [a small Iyland namitt in Erisch] *Ellan nagavna.*

[23] ane rockie knobe *BM.*

[30. *31.*] Narrest this lyis ane Ile callit *Luyng*, 3 myle lang, lyand from the south-west to the north-eist 2 part myle breid with an paroche kirk, gude mane land inhabite and manurit [guid for store and corne its possesit] be M^c^gillane of Doward in feall fra my Lord of Argile,[24] having sufficient for Hieland galies in it.

[31. *32.*] Narrest this lyis ane Ile callit *Saoill* or *Seill* 3 myle lang half myle breid, lyand from the south-west to the north-eist, inhabite and manurit, gude for store and corn, perteining to my Lord of Argile.[25]

[32. *33.*] Narrest this lyis ane Ile callit *Sevnay*, 2 myle lang, half myle breid [from southwest to northeist], inhabite and manurit, gude for store and girsing, perteining to my Lord of Argile.[25]

[33. *34.*] Narrest this lyis ane [little] Ile callit [in Erisch Leid] *Ellan Slait*, quhairin thair is abundance of skailzie to be wyn.

[34. *35.*] Narrest this lyis ane [sma] Ile [in Erische] callit *Ellan Nagvisog*.

[35. *36.*] Narrest this lyis ane Ile callit [in the Erische Leid] *Ellan Eisdalf*.

[36. *37.*] Narrest this lyis ane Ile callit *Iniskenzie*.

[37. *38.*] Narrest this lyis ane Ile callit [in the Erische Leid] *Ellan anthian.*[26]

[38. *39.*] Narrest this lyis ane Ile [27] callit [in Erische Leid] *Ellan Uderga*.

[24] few fra the Earle of Ergyle *BM*.

[25] the Earle of Ergyle *BM*.

[26] *Buch*. (fol. 9) adds: vocatur Thiana, ab herba frugibus noxia non dissimili Luteæ, nisi quod magis diluto sit colore (called Tian, from an herb noxious to corn, somewhat like guild, but only not of such a bright yellow—Aikman's trans.).

[27] ane uther verey small rocke *BM*.

[39. *40.*] Narrest this lyis [ane Iyle, callit in the Erische Leid] *Ellan* [*Righ*], or in English callit the Kings Ile.

[40. *41.*] Narrest this lyis [ane Ile, or rather a grate craige callit in the Erische Leid] *Ellan duff*, or callit in English the Black Ile.

[41. *42.*] Narrest this lyis [ane iyle callit in the Erische Leid] *Ellan naheglis*, callit in English the Kirk Ile.

[42. *43.*] Narrest this lyis *Ellan Chriarache.*[28]

[43. *44.*] Narrest this lyis [ane Iyle callit in the Erische Leid] *Ellan ard*, callit in English the hich Ile.

[44. *45.*] Narrest this lyis [ane Iyle callit in the Erische Leid] *Ellan Iisall*, callit in English the laich Ile.

[45. *46.*] Narrest this [layes ane Iyle namitt in the Erische Leid] the *Glass Ellan*, callit in English the green Ile.

[46. *47.*] Narrest this lyis the [Iyle which in the Erische Leid is namitt] *Freuch Ellan*, callit in English the heder Ile.

[47. *48.*] Narrest this lyis [aneother which in the Erische Leid is callit] *Ellan na cravich.*

[48. *49.*] Narrest this lyis [ane rockie scabrous Iyle callit in the Erische Leid] *Ellan na gobhar*, callit in English the Gaytis Ile.

[49. *50.*] Narrest this lyis [a verey prey litle sandey Iyle callit in the Erische Leid] *Ellan na gumyn*, callit in Eng. the Conyngis Ile.

[50. *51.*] Narrest this lyis [the iyle callit be the Erisch] *Ellan diamhoin*, callit in Eng. the Idle Ile.

[51. *52.*] [Narrest this isle lyes *Eisell ellan* or the laich isle a laich small isle.] [29]

[28] 'C' written over initial letter ; Triaracha *Buch.* ; Chrearache *BM.*
[29] *sec. manu*, as in *BM* ; not in *Buch.*

[52. *53.*] Narrest this lyis *Ellan Abhridich* in Irish Uridithe.

[53. *54.*] Narrest this lyis *Lismoir* ane fair mane Ile 8 myle lang from the north-eist to the south-west, 2 myle braid, with ane paroche kirk quhilk sumtime was the cathedrall kirk seat of the Bischop of Argyle, inhabite and manurit with ane castell callit Achaadn or Bell buacheir, all full of lyme stanes and mettal and leid ovir lyand foiranent Doward.[30]

[54.] Narrest this lyis *Ellan na gaorach,* callit in English the Scheip Ile, 2 myle lang, half myle braid, fertile and fruitfull, inhabite and manurit.

[55.] Narrest this lyis *Suina* 2 myle lang from the north-eist to the south-west, half myle braid, inhabite and manurit.

[56.] Narrest this lyis *Iuichair* callit the Ferray Ile half myle lang, gude for corn store and fisching and girsing also.

[57.] Narrest this lyis *Garbh Ellan,* callit in English Roch Ile, gude for store corn and fisching.

[58.] Narrest this lyis *Ellan Cloich* callit in English the Ile of the stane, gude for store, corn and girsing.

[59.] Narrest this lyis *Flada,* gude for corn, store and fisching.

[60.] Narrest this lyis *Grezay,* gude for corn, store and fisching.

[61.] Narrest this lyis *Ellan Moir,* callit the great Ile, gude for store and corn.

[30] *BM* simply say : Lismoir ane Iyle quher Leid ure is fornent Douard this Iyle is foure myle Lange with ane paroche kirke in it. *Buch.* (fol. 9) says : Lismora, in qua olim sedes Episcopalis Argatheliæ fuerat, longa octo millia P. lata duo. In ea præter communia cum cæteris commoda, metalla inueniuntur (Lismore, eight miles long, and two broad, which was formerly the seat of the bishop of Argyle, and in which, besides the productions common to the others, metals have been found—Aikman's trans.).

[62.] Narrest this lyis *Ardiasgar*, gude for corn, store and fisching.

[63.] Narrest this lyis *Musadill*, half myle lang, gude for corn and fisching.

[64.] Narrest this lyis *Berneray* ane myle lang from the north-eist to the south-west, alsmekle braid, inhabite and manurit, gude for store, with ane wood of Ew in it. This Ile was callit sumtime an holy Girth, very good for scheip.

[65.] Narrest this lyis *Ellan Inhologasgyr*, full of pasture for store and full of rampis.

[66.] *Ellan drynachai* half myle lang, with mekle bourtrie and thornis, with auld mansis, quhair habitation of Bischops and Nobles were in auld times; gude for corn and store.

[67.] *Ransay* gude for corn and store, with mony thornis and bourtrie.

[68.] Narrest this lyis *Ellan Bhellnagobhan*, callit in English the Smith towns Iles, gude for store, with mekle wood.

[69.] Narrest this lyis *Kerveray* 3 myle lang, mair nor half myle braid, gude fertile fruitfull land, inhabite and manurit, very gude for store, perteining to M^c^covle of Lorn.

[70. *55.*] Narrest this forsaid Diuray on the west side of the same lyis *Ila*, ane Ile of 20 myle lang from the north to the south, and 16 myle braid from the eist to the west, fertil fruitfull and full of natural girsing pasture with mony great deiris, mony woods, with fair games of hunting besides every town, with mekle leid ovir [31] in Moychaolis, with ane water callit Laxan whereupon mony salmond are slane, with ane salt-water Loch there callit Loch Gruynord, quhairin runs the waiter of Grunord with haich sandy banks, upon the quhilk banks upon Eb sea lyis infinite

[31] wre *B*, ure *M*.

selchis quhilks are slane with doggis leirnit to the same effect. In this Ile thair is ane gude raid for schippis callit Pollmoir in Irish, and in English the meekle pool. This lyis at ane town callit Lantay vanych. Ane uther Ile [32] lyis within Ellan Ruidard [33] callit in English the Ile of point of the Ness. The rade is callit Leodannus [within this Iyle there is sundrie fresche water Lochis sic as] Loch Moyburg, quhairin thair lyis an Ile perteining to the Bishops of the Iles. The Loch of Ellan thairin,[34] quhairin thair is ane Ile perteining to M^c^gillane of Doward; Loch Sterotsa [35] with ane Ile perteining to the Abbot of Icolmkill. In this Ile thair is strynthie castells: the first callit Dunavaig biggit on ane craig at the sea side on the south-eist part of the cuntrey perteining to the Clan-donald of Kintyre. The second callit the castell of Lochgvrme, quhilk is biggit in ane Ile in the said fresch water loch far fra land perteining to Clan-donald of Kintyre of auld, now usurpit be M^c^gillane of Doward. Ellan Finlagan in the middis of Ila ane fair Ile in fresh water Loch.[36] Into this Ile of Finlagan the Lords of the Iles, quhen thai callit thame selfis Kings of the Iles,

[32] raid *BM*.

[33] ? Rindard ; Ruidarde *B*, Grynord *M*.

[34] Ellan Charrin *BM*.

[35] Loch Cherolsa *BM*.

[36] From 'Loch' (inclusive) to end of paragraph not in *BM*. *Buch*. (fol. 9) says : Præteria aquæ dulcis lacum, in quo est insula Falangama dicta, olim omnium Insulanorum regia, in qua insularum Regulus assumpto nomine regio solebat habitare. Huic propinqua, sed minor est insula Rotunda : cui etiam a consilio nomen est inditum. In ea enim curia erat, in qua quatuordecim e primoribus ius assidue dicebant, ac de summa rerum etiam agitabant consilia : quorum summa æquitas, & moderatio pacem domi, forisque præstitit, & pacis comitem rerum omnium affluentiam (There is also a fresh water loch, wherein stands the island named Falingania, some time the chiefe seat of all the isles men. There the governour of the isles, usurping the name of king, was wont to dwell. Neere unto this island, and somewhat lesse than it, is the Round Island, taking the name from Counsell, for therein was the justice seat, and fourteene of the most worthy of the countrie did minister justice unto all the rest continually, and intreated of the waighty affaires of the realme in counsell, whose great equitie and discretion kept peace both at home and abroad ; and with peace was the companion of peace, abundance of all things—Monipennie's translation).

had wont to remain oft in this Ile forsaid to thair counsell: for thai had the Ile well biggit in palace-wark according to thair auld fassoun, quhairin thai had ane fair chapell. Besides this Ile be ane pennystane cast till it thair is ane uther Ile sumquhat les, fair and round, quhairin thai had thair Counsellhouse biggit, throw the quhilk the said Ile is callit in Irish Ellan na comharle, and in English is callit the Counsell-Ile. In this Ile thair conveinit 14 of the Iles best Barons, that is to say, four greatest of the Nobles callit Lords; to wit M^c^gillane of Doward, M^c^gillane of Lochbuy, M^c^cloyde of Saray,[37] and M^c^cloyde of Leozus. Thir four Barons forsaid might be callit Lords, and were haldin as Lords at sic time. Four Thanes of les living and estate; to wit, M^c^ginnihin,[38] M^c^naie, M^c^neill of Gighay and M^c^neill of Barray. Uther four great men of living of thair royall blude of Clan-donald lineally descendit; to wit Clan-donald of Kintyre, M^c^ane of Ardnanmirquhame, Clan-Ronald, and Clan-Alister Carryche in Lochaber; with the Bishop and the Abbot of Icolmkill. Thir 14 persons sat down into the Counsell-Ile, and decernit, decreitit and gave suits furth upon all debaitable matters according to the Laws made be Renald M^c^Somharkle callit in his time King of the Occident Iles, and albeit thair Lord were at his hunting or at ony uther games, zit thai sate every ane at thair Counsell ministring justice. In thair time thair was great peace and welth in the Iles throw the ministration of justice. In Ila thair is four paroche kirks, to wit Killmheny, Kilmorvin in the middis of the cuntrey, Kilchomain ane fair paroche kirk. In the town of Kilchomain the Lords of the Iles dwelt ofttymes. The kirk of Kildalltan lyand at the south side of the heichest hills in Ila. Ben Cargadh, Corben ben bhayne. This Ile perteinis to Clan-donald of Kintyre now pairtlie, and pairtlie to M^c^gillane of Doward, with ane Falcon-nest in it.

[37] Initial letter changed to 'H' *sec. manu.*
[38] ? M^c^ginmhyn.

[71. *56.*] At the Mouth of the Kyle of Ila betwixt it and Diuray lyis ane Ile callit *Ellan charne*[39] and in English the Ile of Cairick.

Here begin we to cirkell[40] Ila sungaittis aboute with litle Iles, as followis.

[72. *57.*] Narrest this southwart lyis ane Ile callit *Ellan na caltin*, callit in English the Hesill Isle.

[73. *58.*] Narrest that at the said schoir of Ila lyis [ane litle Iyle] *Ellan McMullynory* callit in English mullinoris Ile.

[74. *59.*] Narrest this at the said schoir lyis *Ellan Osrum*[41] southwart.

[75. *60.*] Narrest this at the said schoir southwart lyis *Ellan bryd* callit in English Brydis Ile.

[76. *61.*] Narrest this at the said schoir lyis ane little Ile callit *Corsker*, callit in English the stay skeray or craig.

[77. *62.*] Narrest this at the said schore lyis ane [small] Ile callit *Ellan Isall*,[42] callit in English the laich Ile.

[78. *63.*] Narrest this lyis [the litle] *Ellan Imersga*.

[79. *64.*] Narrest this lyis *Ellan Nabeathi*.

[80. *65.*] Narrest this at the south coist of Ila lyis ane Ile callit *Ellan teggsay* ane myle lang, gude mane land with ane Kirk in it, very gude for scheip and for fisching.

[81. *66.*] Narrest this lyis *Ellan na calrach*, callit in English the Scheips Ile, quhilk is very gude for the same and for corn also.

[39] 'char . .' certain, remainder overwritten; charne *BM*; *Buch.* (fol. 9) says: Inter Ilam, & Iuram sita est insula parua a cumulo lapidum cognominata (Betwixt Isla and Jura, lyes a little island, taking the name from a cairne of stones—Monipennie's trans.).

[40] Overwritten; previously 'with Sircill'.

[41] Ofrum *BM.*

[42] Isallach *sec. manu*; Eisillache *BM.*

[82. *67.*] Narrest this lyis southwart *Ellan na naosg* callit in English the Myresnyppis Ile.

[83. *68.*] Narrest this lyis *Ellan Rinard* [43] callit in English the Ile of the Ness point.

[84. *69.*] Narrest this lyis *Liach Ellan* callit in English the Lyart Ile.

[85. *70.*] Narrest this lyis *Tarskeray.*

[86. *71.*] Narrest this lyis ane Ile callit *Auchnarra.*[44]

[87. *72.*] Narrest this lyis *Ellan moir* callit in English the great Ile, gude for store [and pastourage].

[88. *73.*] Narrest this lyis *Ellan dealloch dune* callit in English the Ile of the manis figure.

[89. *74.*] Narrest this lyis *Ellan Ean* [45] callit in English John his Ile.

[90. *75.*] Narrest this lyis *Ellan stagbadis.*

[91. *76.*] Narrest this lyis at the west point of Ila ane Ile callit *Oversay* ane mile of lenth, with ane Kirk [46] in it, gude land, verie gude for fisching, inhabite and manurit, with ane richt dangerous kyle and stream, callit Corie garnagh.[47] Na man dare enter in it, but at ane certain time of the tide, or else he man perish. This Ile lyis in lenth from the south-eist to the north-west.

[92. *77.*] Narrest this Ile [one the northwest coist of Ila] lyis ane Ile callit *Keanichis Ile* callit in English the Merchandis Ile.

[43] ryndnahard *BM* ; Rinarda *Buch.*
[44] ? Anchnarra ; Achnarra *Buch.*, *BM.*
[45] Overwritten, but probably unchanged.
[46] ane paroche kirke *BM* ; but see *O.P.S.* ii 274 note.
[47] 'n' of 'garnagh' overwritten ; Garraoche *M.*

[93. *78.*] Narrest this lyis ane Ile on the said north-west coist of Ila callit *Usabrast* gude for girs and fishing.

[94. *79.*] Narrest this [one the north coist of Iyla] lyis ane Ile callit *Ellan tanast.*[48]

[95. *80.*] Narrest this lyis *Ellan nefe* on the north coist of Ila besides the enteres of Loch Grinord foirsaid, with ane Kirk in it. The Ile fair mane land, half mile lang, inhabite and manurit, gude for fisching.

[96. *81.*] Narrest this lyis ane Ile callit *Ellan na bany,* callit in English the Webstaris Ile.

[97. *82.*] Narrest this north fra Ila lyis ane Ile callit *Orvansay,* ane Ile of twa mile lang and neir alsmekle braid, quhairin thair is ane Monasterie of Channonis, mane laich land, full of hairis and fowmartis, with gude heavin for hieland Galayis and scheald at the schoiris. This Ile lyis aucht mile of sea northwart from Ila.

[98. *83.*] Narrest this before the Ile of Orvansay lyis ane Ile les nor it callit *Ellan na muk,* half mile lang, quhilk is gude for swine and uther bestiall.

[99. *84.*] North fra the Ile of Orvansay be ane half mile of sea lyis ane Ile callit *Colvansay* seven mile lang from the north-eist to the south-west, with twa mile breid, ane fertile Ile, gude for quhyte fishing, with ane paroche Kirk. This Ile is bruikit be ane gentle Capitane callit Mcduffyhe and perteinit to Clan-donald of Kintyre of auld.

[100. *85.*] Twelff mile northwart from the Ile of Colvansay lyis the Ile of *Mule,* ane great roch Ile; not the les it is fertile and fruitfull. This conteins in lenth from the north-eist to the south-west 24 mile, and in breid fra the eist south-eist to the north north-west [49] uther 24 mile, with

[48] taneste *sec. manu,* as in *BM*; Tanasta *Buch.*

[49] west northwest *BM.*

certane woods, mony deiris and [verey] fair hunting games, with mony great montanes and cordis for hunting, with ane gude raid foiranent Icolmkill callit Polcarf. In this Ile thair is sevin paroche kirks and 3 Castells; to wit, the Castell of Doward ane strenthie place biggit on ane craig at the sea side, the Castell of Lochbury perteining to M^c^gillane of Lochbuy, the Castell of Aross, quhilk sumtime perteinit to the Lords of the Iles, and now is bruikit be M^c^gillane of Doward foirsaid. In this Ile thair is twa gude [freche] waters callit Avinva [50] and the water of Glenforsay full of salmond with sum uther waters that hes salmond on thame, but not in sic abundance of salmond as the waters foirsaid hes on thame, with certane salt water Lochs; to wit Loch Laois,[51] ane little small Loch with gude tak of hering in it. This Loch lyis in the south-west of the cuntry. Next this Loch Leafan,[52] gude tak of hering in it. Northwart fra that Loch lyis Loch Stafart [53] gude for hering. On the eist of the cuntrey lyis ane Loch callit Lochspelf.[54] Narrest this Loch in the south south-eist lyis Lochbuy, ane fair braid Loch with ane gude tak of hering and uther fischingis. Within this Ile thair is twa freshwater Lochis: the ane is callit Loch strat stuaban,[55] with ane Ile upon it callit Ellan strat stuaban [56]; the uther Lochba, with ane Ile upon it. Thir Iles are laich inhabite and strenthis. This Ile perteinis pairtlie to M^c^gillane of Doward, pairtlie to M^c^gillane of Lochbuy, pairtlie to M^c^kinvin, and pairtlie to the Clan-donald of auld. This Ile lyis not four mile fra the ferme land of Morvarne.

[101. *86.*] At the south-west schoir of the Ile of Mule lyis ane little Ile callit *Ellan challmain*, callit in English the Dowis

[50] Avan-va *BM*.
[51] Loch-ear *BM*.
[52] Loche-fyne *BM*.
[53] Loche Scaforte *BM*.
[54] Lochepelst *BM*.
[55] Loche Strathscuban *B*, Strathsenaban *M*.
[56] Ellan Strathsnaban *BM*.

Ile, inhabite and manurit, half mile lang, fruitfull for corn and girsing, with ane heavin for hieland boats, perteining to M^c^gillane of Doward.

[102. *87.*] North-west fra this Ile lyis *Ellan Eray*, ane Ile of uther half mile lang, with ane mile narrest of breid, inhabite and manurit, gude mane land for corn store and [pastorage with aboundance of] fishing.

[103. *88.*] Narrest this be twa mile of sea lyis ane Ile callit in Irish leid *Icholum chille*, that is to say in English Saint Colms Ile, ane fair mayne Ile, of twa mile lang, mair nor ane mile breid, fertile and fruitfull for corn, store and fisching. Within this Ile thair was an Abbay [57] of Monks and ane Monasterie of Nunnis with ane paroche kirk, with sundrie uther chapells dotit of auld be the Kings of Scotland and be the Clan-donald. This Abbay foirsaid was the Cathedral Kirk that the Bischoppis of the Iles had sen the time thai were banist out of the Ile of man be the Inglismen: for within this Ile of Man was thair Cathedral Kirk and thair living and thair dwelling als, as is foirsaid. Within this Ile of Colmkill thair was ane Sanctuarie or Kirkzaird callit in Irish Religoran, quhilk is ane fair Kirkzaird, well biggit about with stane and lyme. Into this Sanctuarie thair is three Tombs of stanes formit like little chapellis with ane braid gray [marble or] quhin stane in the gavill of ilk ane of the Tombs. In the stane of the mid Tomb [58] thair is writtin [in Latin letters] *Tumulus Regum Scotiæ*, that is to say, the Tomb or the Grave of the Scottis Kings. Within this Tomb, according to our Scottis and Irish Chronicles, thair lyis 48 crownit Scottis Kings, throw the quhilk this Ile has bene richlie dotit be the Scottis Kings, as we have hard. The Tomb on the south side of this foirsaid Tomb hes the subscription, to wit, *Tumulus Regum*

[57] monastery *BM.*
[58] the ane tombe *BM* ; qui medius est *Buch.* fol. 10.

Hiberniæ, that is to say, the Tomb of the Irland Kingis: for we have in our Irish Chronicles that thair wes four Irland Kingis eirdit into the said Tomb. Upon the north side of our Scottis Tomb the inscription beiris *Tumulus Regum Norvegiæ*, that is, the Tomb of the Kingis of Norway. In the quhilk Tomb we find in our ancient Irish Chronicles their lyis aucht Kingis of Norway. And als we find in our Irish Chronicles that Coelus King of Norway comandit his Nobles to tak him to Colmkill to be bureit, if it chansit him to die in the Ile[s]. But he was sa discomfite, that thair remanet not of his Army sa mony as wald bury him there: therefore he was bureit in Kyle, efter he strak a feild against the Scottis and wes vincust be thame, as our Albin Scottis Chronicles beiris. Within this Sanctuarie also lyis for the maist [pairt of] the Lords of the Iles with thair linages, tuay Clane lane with thair linages, M^c^kinvin and M^c^guare with thair linage, with sundrie uther inhabitants of the haill Iles, because this Sanctuarie wes wont to be the sepulture of the best men of all the Iles, and als of our Kingis, as we have said; because it wes the maist honorable and ancient place that wes in Scotland in those dayis, as we reid.

[104. *89.*] At the south-west end of this Ile of Colmkill lyis ane Ile callit *Soa*, quhairin thair is infinite number of wild fowl nests, half mile lang, gude for scheip, perteining to Colmkill.

[105. *90.*] On the south-eist of this foirsaid Colmkill lyis ane Ile callit in Irish *Ellan namban*, and in Inglis the Women-Ile, gude for store, fishing and heder, perteining to Colmkill.

[106. *91.*] On the north north-eist end of Colmkill lyis ane little Ile callit *Ellan murudhain*, ane little laich mane [sandey] Ile, gude for scheip and for bent in time of zeir, perteining to Colmkill.

[107. *92.*] On the west north-west of this Ile of Colmkill lyis a little Ile callit *Ellan Reryng* ane profitable Ile of wild fowls eggis and for fisching, perteining to Colmkill.

[108. *93.*] On the north north-eist of this Colmkill lyis ane Ile be twelf mile of sea till it within the enteres of Loch stafart foirsaid callit *Iniskenzie*, uther half mile lang, les nor ane mile breid, ane fair Ile, fertile and fruitfull, inhabite and manurit, full of conyngis about the schoiris of it, with ane paroche kirk, the maist pairt of the parochin being upon the mane schoir of Mule foirsaid, ane half mile distance of sea fra the said Ile. This Ile pertenit to the Prior [59] of Colmkill, and the haill parochin of it.

[109. *94.*] Within this Ile of Iniskenzie in the said Loch of Stafart be ane mile of sea lyis ane Ile callit *Eorsay*, ane fertile Ile, full of corn, girsing and murens, ane mile lang, perteining to the Priore [60] of Colmkill.

[110.] Be twa mile of sea fra this Ellan of Eorsay lyis ane Ile to the north-west callit *Ulvay* five mile lang, gude land with ane gude Raid for hieland galeis in it.

[111.] Before this Ile of Ulvay on the south coist of it lyis ane little Ile callit *Colvansay*, gude land for sa mekle with sum hesill wood in it, and is manurit also.

[112.] Be ane quarter mile of sea to the west north-west fra this Ulvay lyis ane Ile callit *Gomatra* two mile lang from the south to the north, with half mile breid, with twa fair Raidis in it; ane of them on the north side, the best in the south side, gude for mayne schippis to ride on anker; gude land and weill plenishit in corn and girsing.

[113.] Narrest this Gomatra be four mile of sea to the south lyis ane Ile callit *Stafay* half mile lang, abundante

[59] Priores *BM.*
[60] Prioress *sec. manu*, as in *BM.*

of girsing of the meklevine, gude heavin for hieland Galayis, utter fyne for storme and symmer and wynter scheling also.

[114.] Fra this Ile four miles of sea to the west north-west lyis twa Kerniborgis; the ane callit *Kerniborg moir*, the uther callit *Kerniborg beg*; baith strenthie craigis be nature biggit in the sea, and fortifeit about be the devise of man, lyand in the middis of it great stark streams of the sea, bruikit be M^c^gillane of Doward, very perillous for schippis be reason of the starknes of the stream. Thir Craigis are easily made unwynable be craftie men, and namelie the greatest is strenthie but douth.

[115.] Narrest thir Iles be ane mile of sea to the west lyis ane Ile callit *Ellan na monadh*; that is to say in Inglish, the fewall Ile quhilk furdis fewall to the strenthis foirsaid. Some manurit land in it, the rest of mure for fewall 2 pairt myle lang from the eist to the west, with a gude hieland heavin in it.

[116.] Narrest this lyis *Lungay* ane Ile of twa mile of lenth, gude for store, corn and fishing.

[117.] Narrest this lyis to the west south-west ane Ile callit the *Bak*, ane mile lang, very gude for store, namelie for stwidis, and als for fishing.

[118.] Narrest this toward the west be sax mile of the sea lyis *Thiridh* ane mane laich fertile fruitfull cuntrie, aucht mile lang from the north-eist to the south-west; three mile braid from the north-west to the south-eist. All inhabite and manurit with twa paroche kirkis in it, ane fresh water loch, with ane auld castell. Na cuntrie may be mair fertile of corn, and very gude for wild fowls and for fische, with ane gude heavin for heiland galayis.

[119.] Be twa mile of sea from this Ile lies ane Ile callit *Gunna*, ane mile lang from the eist to the west, manurit and inhabite, gude for corn, store and fishing.

[120.] Be twa mile of sea northwart from Gunna lyis ane Ile of half a mile lang callit *Coll* tending in lenth from the south-west to the north-eist and twa mile braid. Ane mane fertile Ile inhabite and manurit, with ane castell and ane paroch kirk in it, gude for fishing and fowlers, with ane utter fine Falcons nest in it.

[121. *95.*] Upon the north north-eist coist of Mule lyis ane Ile callit *Calf*, ane mile lang, full of woods, sufficient raid for schippis perteining to M^c^gillane of Doward.

[122. *96.*] Befor the castell of Aross foirsaid lyis twa Iles; the ane *Glass Ellan moir*, the uther *Glass Ellan beg*; and the south-eist fra that throw the Kyle of Mule lyis twa Iles of the foirsaid twa names perteining to M^c^gillane of Doward.

[123. *97.*] From these Glass Ellans to the south-eist lyis ane Ile callit *Ellan Ardan ridir*, callit in Inglis the Knytis Ile, or the Ile of the Knytis Ness perteining to M^c^gillane of Doward.

[124. *98.*] Southwart from Dowart lyis ane Ile upon the schoir side callit in Irish *Ellan amhadi*, and in Inglis the Wolfis Ile, gude for store, [being bentey] perteining to M^c^gillane of Doward.

[125. *99.*] Southwart from Ellan amhadi upon the schore of Mule lyis ane Ile callit *Ellan moir*, gude for store and for fisching perteining to M^c^gillane of Lochbuy.

[126. *100.*] Sixteen mile northwart fra the Ile of Coll lyis ane Ile callit *Rum*, ane Ile of 16 mile lang, 6 mile braid, in the neirest ane forrest full of heich montanes and abundante of little deiris in it, quhilk deiris will never be slane down-with but the principall settis man be in the heich of the hills, because the deir will be callit upwart ay be tynchellis, or without tynchellis they will up a forte.[61] In this Ile thair

[61] will pas upwart perforce *BM.*

will be gottin about Beltane [62] als mony wild fowl nestis full of eggis about the murc [63] as men pleases to gadder, and that becaus the fowls hes few to start thame except deiris. This Ile stands fra the west to the eist in lenth, and perteins to the Laird of Coll callit M^c^ane abrie. Mony solenne geis are in this Ile. This land obeyis to M^c^gillane of Doward instantlie.

[127. *101.*] Be four mile of sea towards the south-eist lyis ane little Ile half mile lang callit in Irish *Ellan na neach*, callit in Inglish the horse Ile, gude for horse and uther store, perteining to the Bischop of the Iles.

[128. *102.*] Be ane half mile of sea to this foirsaid Ile lyis ane Ile of twa mile lang, callit in Irish *Ellan na muk*, and in Inglish the Swines Ile, ane verie fertile frutfull Ile of cornis and girsing for all store, verie gude for fische, inhabite and manurit, with ane gude falcon nest, perteining to the Bischop of the Iles; with ane gude hieland heavin in it, the entrie at the west cheek of it.

[129. *103.*] Be twa mile of sea towards the north-west from this foirsaid Rum lyis ane Ile callit *Cannay*, fair mane land, four mile lang inhabite and manurit, with an paroch kirk in it, gude for corn, girsing and fisching, with an falcon nest in it. It perteins to the Abbot of Colmkill.

[130. *104.*] North fra this Ile callit Ellan na muk be four mile lyis ane Ile callit *Egge*, four mile lang, twa mile braid, gude mayne land, with ane paroch kirk in it, with mony solenne geis; very gude for store, namelie for scheip, with ane heavin for hieland Galayis.

[62] Beltane *B*, Bretane *M*; *Buch.* (fol. 10) says: quia raris in locis habitata est, aues marinæ passim in campis oua ponunt, quorum quantum libet quiuis *vere* adulto colliget (Being only inhabited in a few places, the sea fowl every where in the fields, deposite their eggs, of which any quantity may be collected *in the spring*—Aikman's trans.).

[63] maney wyld foulls nests upone the plaine mure *BM* (*M* omits 'foulls').

F

[131. *105.*] North-eist fra this foirsaid Ile of Rum be twelf mile of sea lyis ane Ile uther half mile lang callit *Soabretill*, ane roche Ile quhairin deiris uses to be and hunting games, perteining to M^c^cloyde of Herey.

[132. *106.*] North fra this be twa miles of sea lies the great Ile of *Sky* tending fra the south to the north to 42 miles, roch and lang; that is to say, fra the south point of Slait to the north point of Trouterness [64]; and 8 mile braid [in some places] and in uther places 12 mile braid. In this Ile thair is 12 paroch kirks, inhabite and manurit fertile land, namely for aittis, excelland ony uther ground for girsing and pasture, abundante of store and of stwidis.[65] In it mony woods, mony forrests, [maney deire], fair hunting games, mony great hillis, principallie Cwillvelum and Glamok. Within this Ile thair is gude tak of salmond fische upon five principall wateris; to wit, the water of Snersport, the water of Sliggacham, the water of Straitsnarsdill, the water of Linlagallan,[66] and the water of Killmartine, and seven or aucht uther small waters, quhairupon smaller salmond fische are slain. In this Ile thair is ane fresh water Loch, quhairupon thair is slane salmond and kipper callit the Loch of Glenmoir. Within this thair is five castles; to wit, the Castle of Dunvegane perteining to M^c^cloyde of Hary, ane stark strenth biggit on ane craig; the Castell of Dumakin perteining to M^c^kinvin; the Castell Dunringill perteining to the said M^c^kynvin, the Castell of Cames in Slait perteining to Donald Gormesoun; and the Castell of Duntvillmen perteining to the said Donald Gormesoun within Trouternes: and the Castell of Dunskayt in Slait perteining to the said Donald Gormesoun. Within this Ile thair is seven sundrie cuntreys; to wit Slait perteining to Donald Gormesoun; Stratsnordill perteining to M^c^kynvin, quhilk lyis next Slait ; Mengzenes perteining to M^c^cloyd

[64] ? Tronterness, as in *B* ; Trouternesse *M.*
[65] stuidds *B*, studds *M.*
[66] Ranlagallan *BM.*

of Haray; Braakadill perteining to the said M^c^cloyd; Denrynes [67] perteining to the said M^c^cloyd; Waternes perteining to M^c^cloyd of Leozus; and Trouternes [68] perteining to Donald Gormesoun. Into this Ile thair is three principall salt water Lochis; to wit, Loch Sliggachan, Loch Synort,[69] and Loch Slaopan: gude tak of hering in thir three Lochis. By thir three Lochis, thair is within this Ile 13 salt water Lochis; to wit, Loch Stafayk, Loch Emort, Loche Vrakdill, [Loche] Kensale, Herlois, Loch Dunvegane, Loch Gristrins, Loch Arnossort, Loch Wge, Loch Sneisport, Loch Portrigh, [Loche] Kenloch na-daladh in Slait [70]: gude tak of hering in mony of thir Lochis [sometymes bot nought sa guid by far as in the 3 first Loches]. This Ile is callit Ellan Skianach in Irish, that is to say in Inglish the wyngit Ile, be reason it hes mony wyngis and pointis lyand furth fra it, throw the deviding of thir foirsaid Lochis.

[133. *107.*] About this Ile of Sky thair lyis in ane circle certane Iles; to wit, at the coist side of Slait lyis ane Ile callit *Orandsay* ane mane land, inhabite and manurit gude land; perteining to Donald Gormesoun.

[134. *108.*] Foiranent Loch Ailis lyis ane Ile callit in Irish *Ellan Naguyneyne*, that is to say in Inglish the Conyng Ile, full of wood and conyngis, half mile lang, perteining to M^c^kenzie of Kintaill.

[135. *109.*] At the schoir of the Strat foirsaid lyis ane Ile callit *Pabay* west [neire] ane myle lang, full of woods, gude for fisching, and for thieves [71] to await on leill mennis geir, perteining to M^c^kynvin.

[67] ? Deurynes.

[68] ? Tronternes.

[69] Downort *B*, Lownort *M*.

[70] *BM* list the following Lochs : Skahauaik/Skahanaik, Emorte, Vrakdill, Kensale-serloss, Dunbegan, Gorsarinis, Arnossort, Snasporte, Portri, Ken, Nadalae in Sleitt, adding, 'The uther tua Loches my memorey is fayled of them'.

[71] and a maine shelter for theeives and cutthrotts *BM*.

[136. *110.*] Fra this Ile of Pabay south-west [72] be aucht mile of sea lyis ane Ile callit *Scalpay*, four mile lang, alsmekle braid, and fair hunting forrest full of deir, and certane little woods with certane towns, inhabite and manurit, with strenthie coves, gude for fisching, perteining to M^c^gillane of Doward in heritage.

[137. *111.*] Betwixt the mouth of Loch Caron and Raarsay lyis *Crowling* [ane small ile zea rather a] gude raid for schippis.

[138. *112.*] Twa mile of sea fra this Ile of Scalpay foirsaid northwart lyis ane Ile callit *Raarsay* seven mile lang from the south to the north, lyand but ane mile of sea from Trouternes, twa mile of breid, with pairt of birkin woods, mony deir, pairt of profitable land, inhabite and manurit; with twa castellis, to wit, the castell of Kilmaluok [73] and the castell of Brerkdill; with twa fair orcheartis at the saidis twa castellis; with ane paroche kirk callit Kilmaluok [74]; ane roche cuntrie, but all full of frie stanes and gude querrellis, gude for fisching, perteining to M^c^gillichallum of Raarsay be the sword, and all to the Bischop of the Iles in heritage. This M^c^gillichallum sould obey M^c^cloyd of Leozus.

[139. *113.*] At the north end of this foirsaid Ile of Raarsay be ane half mile of sea fra it lyis ane Ile callit *Ronay*, mair nor ane mile lang, full of wood and hedder, with a heavin for hieland Galeis in the middis of it. And the said heavin is quiet for fostering of thieves, ruggaris and reevaris till await upon the pailing and spuilzeing of poor mens geir, perteining to M^c^gillichallum of Raarsay be force and to the Bischop of the Iles be heritage.

[140. *114.*] *Ellan Gerloch* in the mouth of Gerloch: in it is gude raid for schippis.

[72] north west *BM* (more correctly).
[73] ? Kilmalnok ; Kilmorocht *BM*.
[74] ? Kilmalnok ; Kilmolowocke *BM*.

[141. *115.*] To the north fra Ronay be six mile of sea lyis ane Ile callit *Fladay*, ane meane roch Ile, half mile lang, inhabite and manurit, fruitfull in corn and girsing, perteining to Donald Gormsoun.

[142. *116.*] Narrest this Fladay be twa myle of sea at the schoir of Trouternes lyis ane Ile callit *Ellan Tuylmen* half mile lang or thairby, manurit, gude for corn and store, perteining to Donald Gormsoun.

[*117.*] [Foure myle of sea fra this Ile Twilin northwart lyes ane Ile callit .]

[143. *118.*] Upon the south side of Sky be ane half mile to the schoir of Braakadill foirsaid lyis ane Ile callit *Orandsay*, half mile lang, ane bonie Ile for corn and girsing, perteining to M^c^cloyd of Haray.

[144. *119.*] Be ane mile of sea to this Ile of Orandsay lyis ane Ile callit *Bwya moir*, gude for corn and store, perteining to M^c^cloyd of Haray.

[145-149. *120-3.*] Betwixt Bwya moir and Ellan Isa lyis five small Iles not mekle of profit.[75]

[150-152. *124-6.*] [Befor the castle of dunbegan lyes 3 small isles.[76]]

[153. *127.*] At the schoir of Waternes lyis ane Ile callit *Ellan Isa*, ane fair laich mayne Ile inhabite and manurit, verie fertile and frutfull for corn and girsing, ane mile lang, half mile braid, havand beside it ane uther laich Ile full of scheip. This Ile is gude for fishing, perteining to M^c^cloyd of Leozus.

[75] Narrest the Ile of Bwya moir Lyes 4 small Iles quhosse Names the author hes Left blankes for *BM*; deinde Buia maior, ac deinceps quinque paruæ insulæ ignobiles *Buch.* fol. 10.

[76] *sec. manu*, as in *BM*; not in *Buch.*

[154. *128.*] On the eist schoir of Waternes lyis ane Ile callit *Ellan Askerin,*[77] abundand of girsing and pasture, mair useit for scheling and store than for corn land, gude for fishing and slauchter of selchis, perteining to M^c^cloyd of Leozus.

[155. *129.*] Upon the schoir of Lindill lyis ane Ile callit *Ellan Lindill*, verie gude for beir and scheip, perteining to M^c^cloyd of Haray.

[156. *130.*] From this Ile of Sky toward the south-west be 80 miles of sea lyis ane Ile callit *Lingay*, gude for girsing and fisching, the Bischop of the Iles lands, ane Ile of half mile lang, with ane falcon nest in it.

[157. *131.*] Bakwart to the north beside the Ile of Lingay is ane Ile callit *Gigarmen*, half mile lang, perteining to the Bischop of the Iles, with ane falcon nest in it.

[158. *132.*] Beside this Ile of Gigarmen towards the north lyis ane Ile callit *Berneray*, verie fertile land, inhabite and manurit, ane mile lang, gude for fishing, perteining to the Bischop of the Iles.

[159. *133.*] Beside the Ile of Berneray towards the north lyis ane Ile callit *Megalay*, twa mile lang, inhabite and manurit, verie gude for corn and fishing, perteining to the Bischop of the Iles.

[160. *134.*] Besides this Ile of Megalay, towards the north north-eist, lyis ane Ile callit *Pabay*, ane mile lang, inhabite and manurit, gude tak of fische in it, perteining to the Bischop of the Iles.

[161. *135.*] Besides this Ile lyis ane Ile to the northwart callit *Fladay*, ane mayne land, frutfull in corn, and als ane [78] fishing, perteining to the Bischop of the Iles.

[77] ? Askerm ; Askerin *BM* ; Askerma *Buch.*
[78] als in *BM.*

[162. *136.*] Besides this Ile of Fladay toward the north lyis ane Ile callit *Scarpay na mult*, twa mile lang, with ane halk nest in it, full of pasture, gude for fishing, perteining to the Bischop of the Iles.

[163. *137.*] Besides this Ile toward the north lyis ane Ile twa mile lang callit *Sanderay*, very gude for corn and fishing, inhabite and manurit, perteining to the Bischop of the Iles.

[164. *138.*] Besides this Ile northwart lyis ane Ile callit *Vatersay*, twa mile lang, ane mile braid, with ane excellent raid for mayne schippis that cumis thair to fische,[79] ane faire mayne Ile, inhabit and manurit, abundand of corn and girsing, gude pasture for scheip for the mekledome of it. All thir nine Iles foirsaid had ane chapell in everie Ile perteining to the Bischop of the Iles.

[165. *139.*] Besides this Ile of Vatersay towards the north, be twa mile of sea, lyis ane Ile callit *Barray*, seven mile lang from the south-west to the north-eist, four mile braid from the south-eist to the north-west; ane fertile and frutfull Ile for corn, and abundante of fisching of keiling, ling, and uther quhyte fisches, with ane paroche kirk callit Kilbaray. Within the south-west end of this Ile thair enteris ane salt water Loch, verie narrow in the entres, and round and braid within. Into the middis of the said Loch thair is ane castell in ane Ile upon ane strenthie craig callit Keselum perteining to M^c^neill of Barray. In the north end of this cuntrey of Barray thair is ane round heich know mayne girs and grene about all to the heid thairof. Upon the heid of this know thair is ane spring and fresh water well. This

[79] Vatersa, quæ præter alia commoda plurima stationem habet multarum, & magnarum nauium capacem, in quam ex omnibus circumiacentibus regionibus statis temporibus magna piscatorum frequentia conuenire solet *Buch.* fol. 10 (Vatersa, which, besides a great many other advantages, possesses a capacious harbour, capable of receiving ships of the largest size, in which a vast number of fishermen assemble at stated seasons, from all the surrounding regions—Aikman's trans.).

well trewlie springis up certane little round quhyte things les nor the quantitie of ane quhyte virne,[80] likest to the shape, figure and form of ane little Cockle as it appeirit to me. Out of this well thair rynnis ane little strype downwith to the sea; and quhair this strype enteris into the sea, thair is ane mile braid of sandis, quhilk ebbis ane mile, callit in Irish the Craimoir[81] of Kilbaray, that is to say in Inglis, the great sandis of Baray. This sandis is all full of great Cockles, and alledgit be the ancient cuntrymen that all thay Cockles cumis down out of the foirsaid hill throw the said strype in the first small form as we have spoken, and eftir thair cuming into the sandis growis great Cockles, the confirmation quhairof I leif to M[r] Hector Boyis. But alwayis thair is not ane fairer and mair profitable sandis for Cockles in ony pairt of the warld. This Ile perteins to M[c]neill of Barray.

[166. *140.*] Betwixt Barray and Vyst thair lyis first *Orbandsay*, half mile lang, with ane falcon nest, ane gude profitable Ile inhabite and manurit, gude for scheip, perteining to M[c]neill of Barray.

[167. *141.*] Besides this lyis *Ellan nahaonchaorach*, callit in Inglish the ane sheip Ile, ane little Ile full of girsing, gude for store, perteining to M[c]neill of Barray.

[168. *142.*] Besides this lyis *Ellan na hakersait*, half mile lang, with ane heavin for hieland galayis, perteining to M[c]neill of Barray.

[169. *143.*] Besides this lyis ane Ile callit *Garvlanga*, ane Ile full of girsing, gude for fisching, perteining to M[c]neill of Barray.

[170. *144.*] Besides this lyis ane Ile callit *Fladay*, half mile lang, with ane falcon nest in it, fertile and frutfull, perteining to M[c]neill of Barray.

[80] ? virn ; corne *sec. manu* ; Conseil [?] Corne *B*, Confeit Corne *M*.
[81] Trayrmore *BM*.

[171. *145.*] Besides this lyis ane Ile callit *Buya beg*, half mile lang, gude for girsing and fisching, perteining to M^c^neill of Barray.

[172. *146.*] Besides this lyis ane Ile callit *Buya moir*, twa mile lang, manurit, full of girsing and pasture, with a falcon nest in it, perteining to M^c^neill of Barray.

[173. *147.*] Besides this lyis ane Ile callit *Hay*, half mile lang, fertile and frutfull, gude for fisching, perteining to M^c^neill of Barray.

[174. *148.*] Besides this lyis ane Ile callit *Hellisay*, ane mile lang, fertile and frutfull, [weill manurit] gude for fisching,[82] perteining to M^c^neill of Barray.

[175. *149.*] Besides this lyis ane Ile callit *Gigay*, ane mile lang, fertile and frutfull, gude for store and fishing, perteining to M^c^neill of Barray.

[176. *150.*] Besides this lyis ane Ile callit *Lingay*, half mile lang, ane verie gude Ile for girsing, pasture and for scheling, perteining to M^c^neill of Barray.

[177. *151.*] Besides this lyis ane Ile callit *Feray*, half mile lang, gude in corn and girsing, and als for fisching, perteining to M^c^neill of Barray.

[178. *152.*] Besides this lyis ane mane sandie Ile callit *Fuday*, verie fertile and frutfull for beir and murens, the quhilk Ile payis murens zeirlie to M^c^neill of Barray for pairt of thair mails and dewteis.

[179. *153.*] To the eist of this Ile of Fuday, be three mile of sea, lyis ane Ile callit *Eriskay*, twa mile lang, inhabite and manurit. In this Ile thair is gottin [dylie] verie abundant of [werey grate] pintill fisch at ebb seais, and als verie gude for uther quhyte fische: perteining to M^c^neill of Barray.

[82] excellent for all sorte of quhyte fishe taking *BM*.

[180. *154.*] Northwart fra this Ile foirsaid lyis the great Ile of *Vyist*, 34 mile lang from the south south-west to the north north-eist, 6 mile braid, ane fertile cuntrie, ane mane laich land, full of heich hills and forrests on the eist coist or south-eist, and all plenishit laich land on the north north-eist,[83] with five paroche kirkis. This cuntrie is bruikit be sundrie Capitanes; to wit, the south south-west end of it callit Vaghastill [84] be Mcneill of Barray. Within his south pairt of Vyist on the eist coist of the same lyis ane salt water Loch callit Loch Wagcastell.[85] The rest of the Ile callit Peiteris parochin, the parochin of Howf, and the mane land of the mid cuntrey callit Matherhanach [85] perteins to Clan-Renald, haldin of the Clan-Donald of Kintyre; and at the end thairof the sea enteris, and cuttis the cuntrie be ebbing and flowing throw it. And in the northside of this thair is ane parochin callit Vlmdbhadhla [86] perteining to the said Clan-Donald. At the north end thereof the sea cuttis the cuntrie agane, and that cutting of the sea is callit the Faghill of Caraness.[87] And be north this the cuntrie is callit kean tuathe [88] of Vyist, that is to say in Inglis, the north heid of Vyist, quhilk conteins to twa paroch kirks, and is mair of profit than the rest of the haill Vyist, pertein-ing to Donald Gormesoun. In this Ile thair is infinite number of fresh water Lochis: but thair is ane [maine] Loch intill it callit Loch Vi [89] three mile lang. Ane arm of the sea hes worn the earth that wes at the tane end of this Loch, quhilk ze sea hes gottin entres to the said fresh water Loch; and in that narrow entres that the sea hes gottin to the said Loch foirsaid the cuntriemen hes biggit up ane thik dyke of great roche stones and penniestane cast lang narrest;

[83] on the northwest *BM.*
[84] Baghastill, Waghastill *BM.*
[85] Machermeanache *BM.*
[86] ? Vlindbhadhla ; Buchagla *BM* ; *cf.* No. 181.
[87] callit Carey-nesse *BM.*
[88] ? tnathe ; Kenchnache *BM.*
[89] Loche-bi *BM.*

notwithstanding the flowing streams of the sea enteris in throw the said dyke of stanes in the said fresh water Loch, and sa thair is gottin amang the roch stanes of the dyke foirsaid flewkis, podlokis, schaytis and little hering stikand fast amang the stanes. Upon this Loch thair is gottin ane kind of fish the quantitie and shape of ane salmond without skaills, the uther [90] half narrest his womb quhyte of it and the u[p]maist half narrest his bak jeat blak, with finnis like ane salmond. Into this north heid of Vyist thair is sundrie coves and holes under the earth coverit with hedder above, quhilk fosteris money rebellis in the cuntrey of the north heid of Vyist, and in the said cuntrie of Vyist thair is sundrie halk nestis.

[181. *155.*] [Betwix the Kentnache and Benvalgha lyes ane werey small Ile callit .[91]]

[182. *156.*] Be aucht mile of sea from this Ile towards the west lyis ane Ile four mile lang, half mile braid, laich mane land, callit *Helsker na caillach,* perteining to the Nunnis of Colmkill, gude corn land not well fyrit.[92]

[183. *157.*] To the north-west of the Keantuach of Vyist lyis ane Ile be 12 mile of sea callit *Haifsker,* quhairin infinite slauchter of selchis is maid at certane times in the zeir, perteining to Donald Gormesoun.

[184. *158.*] To the west north-west of this Ile out of [93] the mane Ocean seais be 60 mile of sea lyis ane Ile callit *Hirta,* mane laich sa far as is manurit of it, abundand in corn and girsing, namelie for scheip, for thai are fairer and greater scheip thair and langer taillit than thair is in ony uther Ile thairabout. The inhabitants thairof are simple

[90] under *BM.*

[91] *sec. manu* (as in *BM*), with a name (Helskernagarlo——) partly obliterated in binding, but this seems to be No. 182.

[92] it hes aboundance of corne and elding for fyre *BM* (incorrect, *cf.* Beveridge, *North Uist,* 324 note).

[93] out in *BM.*

creatures, scant learnit in ony Religion: but M^c^cloyd of Haray his Stewart, or quhom he deputtis in sic office, sayles anes in the zeir at midsymmer with sum chaiplane to baptize bairns thair; and gif they want ane chaiplane, thai baptize thair bairns thameselfis. The said Stewart, as himself tald me, usit to tak ane mask of malt thair with ane maskein fat and mask his malt, and or the fat be readie, the commons of the town baith men, women and bairns puttis thair hand in the fat, and finding it sweit greynes eftir the sweitnes thairof, quhill neither wort nor draff are left unsuppit out thair, quhill baith men, women and bairns were deid drunkin, so that thai could nocht stand on thair feit. The saids Stewartis ressaves thair maillis in maill and reistit muttonis, wild reistit foullis and selchis. This Ile is mair nor ane mile lang narrest, alsmekle breid, quhilk is not seen of ony land or of ony schoir; But at the schoir side of it lyis three great hills, quhilk are ane pairt of Hirt, quhilk are seen far off from the forlands. In thir roch Iles are infinite fair scheippis, with ane falcon nest and wild foullis biggand. But the seais are stark and verie evill entering in ony of the saids Iles. This Ile perteinit to M^c^cloyd of Haray of auld.

[185. *159.*] At the north-west coist of this forsaid Kentuath lyis ane Ile callit *Valay*, twa mile lang from the north to the south, ane mile braid, ane fair mayne Ile, [inhabit and manurit],[94] perteining to Donald Gormesoun.

[186. *160.*] Betwixt this Kentuath and the Harey lyis certane profitable [95] Iles, to wit, *Soa*, inhabite and manurit, ane mile lang, mayne land, perteining to Donald Gormsoun.

[187.] Besides this lyis ane Ile callit *Stroma*, inhabite and manurit, gude land, les nor ane mile lang.

[94] *B*; inhabit *M*.
[95] non infrugiferæ *Buch.* fol. 11.

[188.] Besides this lyis ane maist profitable Ile callit *Pabay*, four mile lang, ane mile braid, maist plentifull of beir, girsing and fisching.

[189.] Besides this lyis ane Ile callit *Berneray* als lang, als braid, als plentifull.

[190.] Besides this lyis ane Ile callit *Enisay*, quhairin M^c^cloyd of Harey hes a dwelling place, ane fair mayne land, weill inhabite and manurit, ane mile lang, half mile braid.

[191.] Beside this lyis ane Ile callit *Keligir*, inhabite and manurit, half mile lang, fertile and frutfull for the mekle-dome.

[192.] Beside this lyis ane Ile callit *Sagha beg*, manurit, fertile and frutfull.

[193.] Beside this lyis ane Ile callit *Sagha moir*, half mile lang, fertile and frutfull, inhabite and manurit.

[194.] Beside this lyis *Hermodray*, half mile lang, fertile and frutfull.

[195.] Beside this lyis *Scarvay*, fertile and frutfull, inhabite and manurit.

[196.] Beside this lyis *Grya*, verie profitable for feiding and fostering of gudes.

[197.] Besides this lyis *Linga*, verie profitable also for feeding and fostering of gudes.

[198.] Beside this lyis *Gillinsay*, inhabite and manurit, verie profitable for girsing and fishing.

[199.] Beside this lyis *Heyia*, verie profitable for girsing and fishing.

[200.] Beside this lyis *Hoya*, verie profitable for store and fishing.

[201.] Besides this lyis *Ferelay*, inhabite and manurit, fertile and frutfull for corn, store and fishing.

[202.] Besides this lyis *Soya beg*, manurit, fertile and frutfull for corn, store and fishing.

[203. *185.*] Besides this lyis ane Ile callit *Soya moir*, manurit, fertile and frutfull, gude for fishing, ane mile lang.

[204. *186.*] Besides this lyis *Ellan Isay*, manurit, fertile and frutfull, gude for fishing.

[205. *187.*] Besides this lyis *Seuna beg*, manurit, fertile and frutfull, gude for corn, store and fishing, half mile lang.

[206. *188.*] Besides this lyis *Seuna moir*, mair nor ane mile lang,[96] half mile braid, inhabite and manurit, gude for corn, store and fishing.

[207. *189.*] Besides this lyis *Tarandsay*, ane Ile of five mile lang, half mile braid, inhabite and manurit; ane roch Ile with certane townis. But all this tilth is delvit with spaidis, except sa mekle as ane hors pleuch will teill; and zit thay have maist abundante of beir, and maist myth of corn,[97] store and fishing; perteining to M^c^cloyd of Haray.

[208. *190.*] Besides this lyis the Ile of *Slegain*, manurit, gude for corn, store and fishing, perteining to M^c^cloyd of Haray.

[209. *191.*] Besides this lyis *Tuemen*, gude for corn, store and fishing, perteining to M^c^cloyd of Haray.

[210. *192.*] Besides this out in the sea above Usiemes in Heray lyis ane Ile callit the *Scarp*, manurit, fertile and frutfull, gude for corn, store and fishing, perteining to M^c^cloyd of Haray.

[211. *193.*] Above the north-west coist of Leozus towards the mayne occident seas lyis certane Iles, of whom I will

[96] an Ile of a myle of lenthe *BM*.
[97] mightie of corne *B* ; mighel of store *M*.

make mention, or we begin Heray and Leozus: to wit, first fiftie mile in the occident seais, from the coist of the parochin of Vige in Leozus, towards the west north-west lyis the 7 Iles of *Flavain*, callit with thame girth and halie Iles,[98] verie naturall girsing. Within thir saidis Iles is infinite wild scheip, quhilks na man knawis quha pat in the said scheip of thame that lives this day of the cuntriemen. But M^c^cloyd of Leozus at certane times in the zeir sendis men and houndis thair, and huntis mony of the said scheip to deid. The flesh of thir scheip may not be eittin be honest and clene men for fatnes: for thair is na flesh on thame but all quhyte like talloun, and wild gustit thairwith. The saidis Iles are nather manurit nor inhabite, but great heich grene hillis full of wild scheip in thai 7 Iles foirsaid quhilk may not be ovircumein, perteining to M^c^cloyd of Leozus.

[212. *194*.] Besides the coist of Leozus towards the said north-west lyis ane Ile callit *Garvellan*, gude for store and fishing, perteining to M^c^cloyd of Leozus.

[213. *195*.] Besides this lyis ane Ile callit *Lambay*, gude also for store and fishing, perteining to M^c^cloyd of Leozus.

[214. *196*.] Besides this lyis *Fladay*, gude for store and fishing, ane bony laich Ile, perteining to M^c^cloyd of Leozus.

[215. *197*.] Besides this lyis *Keallasay*, ane gude Ile, narrest ane mile lang, frutfull for store and fishing, and als manurit, perteining to M^c^cloyd of Leozus.

[216. *198*.] Besides this Keallasay lyis *Berneray beg*, ane half mile lang narrest, mile braid, ane laich roch Ile, full of little laich craigis and holvis [99] betwixt, of naturall fertile earth, and infinite for wair on every schoir of the same. This Ile is weill inhabite and manurit, and will gif zeirlie mair nor 200 bollis beir with delving only, perteining to M^c^cloyd of Leozus.

[98] septem insulæ, quas alij Flauanas, alij Sacras, Asyla vocant *Buch*. fol. 11.
[99] how *BM*.

[217. *199.*] Beside this lyis *Berneray moir*, ane Ile of five mile lang, inhabite and manurit, fertile and frutfull, with mony pastures and mekle store, gude for fishing and fewall also, perteining to M^c^cloyd of Leozus.

[218. *200.*] Besides this lyis *Kirtay*, inhabite and manurit, ane mile lang, fertile and fruitfull, gude for store and fishing, perteining to M^c^cloyd of Leozus.

[219. *201.*] Besides this lyis *Bwya beg*, inhabite and manurit, gude for store, corn and fishing, perteining to M^c^cloyd of Leozus.

[220. *202.*] Besides this lyis *Bwya moir*, mair nor ane mile lang, inhabite and manurit, gude for store, corn and fishing, perteining to M^c^cloyd of Leozus.

[221. *203.*] Besides this lyis *Vexay*, ane gude mane Ile, ane mile lang, inhabite and manurit, verie naturall pastures for store, fishing and fewall, perteining to M^c^cloyd of Leozus.

[222. *204.*] Besides this lyis *Pabay*, ane Ile mair nor ane mile lang, ane frutfull, fertile mane Ile full of corn and scheip, quhairin thair wes a kirk, quhairin also M^c^cloyd of Leozus uses to dwell, quhan he wald be quiet or feirit. This Ile is gude for fishing also, perteining to M^c^cloyd of Leozus.

[223. *205.*] Besides this Pabay lyis *Sigrame moir na guneyne*, that is to say, the great Conyngis Ile, quhairin thair are mony conyngis, gude for girsing and fishing, perteining to M^c^cloyd of Leozus.

[224. *206.*] Besides this lyis *Sigram beg*, manurit, gude for corn, girsing and fishing, half mile lang, perteining to M^c^cloyd of Leozus.

[225. *161.*] At the north point of Leozus thair is ane little Ile callit the *Pygmeis Ile*, with ane little kirk in it of thair awn handie wark. Within this kirk the ancients of the cuntrie of Leozus sayis that the saids Pygmeis hes bene earthit thair. Mony men of divers cuntries hes delvit up deiply the fluir of the said kirk, and I myself amangis the lave, and hes fundin in it deip under the earth certane banes and round heids of verie little quantitie, alledgit to be the banes of the saids Pygmeis, quhilk may be licklie according to sindrie storeis that we reid of the Pygmeis. But I leave this far of it to the ancients of the Leozus. This Ile perteins to M^c^cloyd of Leozus.

In the south-eist coist of Leozus thair enteris twa great salt water Lochis of quhyte fischings; to wit the north Loch of the Y, and the south Loch of the Y. Thir twa Lochis are full of quhyte fische everie time in the zeir, perteining to M^c^cloyd of Leozus.[100]

[226. *162.*] Besides[101] this at the south-eist schoir of Leozus lyis ane Ile callit *Ellan Fabill*, very gude for vayk store and fishing, perteining to M^c^cloyd of Leozus.

[227. *163.*] South fra this said coist lyis *Ellan Adam*, manurit, and gude for vaik bestiall, perteining to M^c^cloyd of the Leozus.

[228. *164.*] Upon the said schoir, towards the west, lyis *Ellan na nuan* callit in Inglish the Lambs Ile, quhairin all the vaik lambs of that end of the cuntrie uses to be fed and fosterit,[102] perteining to M^c^cloyd of the Leozus.

[229. *165.*] Betwix this Ile and Steornvay thair lyis *Ellan Huilmen*, manurit and gude for store and corn, perteining to M^c^cloyd of the Leozus.

[100] This paragraph not in *BM*; In eo litore Leogi insulæ, quod in orientem hibernum spectat duo sinus maris in terram irrumpunt, quorum alterum lacum Meridionalem, alterum Septentrionalem vocant. Vterque toto anno pisces abunde captantibus suppeditat *Buch.* fol. 11.

[101] Besouth *BM*; ad meridiem *Buch.* fol. 11.

[102] fed, and spained fra the zowes *BM*.

[230. *166.*] Southwart fra this Ile lyis *Ellan Viccowill*, ane gude Ile for corn, store and fisching, perteining to M^c^cloyd of the Leozus.

[231. *167.*] Besides this lyis *Havreray*, ane gude Ile for corn, girsing and fisching, ane mile lang, perteining to M^c^cloyd of the Leozus.

[232. *168.*] Besides this lyis *Laxay*, ane gude Ile full of corn, girsing and fishing, perteining to M^c^cloyd of the Leozus.

[233. *169.*] Besides this lyis *Ere*, quhilk is in Inglish callit Irland, laich mane land, full of corn and girsing, perteining to M^c^cloyd of the Leozus.

[234. *170.*] Within the Lochis foirsaid lyis *Ellan Cholmkle* callit in Inglish St Colmis Ile. Within this Ile M^c^cloyd of the Leozus hes ane fair Orcheard, and he that is Gardiner hes that Ile frie; gude mane land for corn, girsing and fishing, perteining to M^c^cloyd of the Leozus.

[235. *171.*] Besides this lyis *Torray*, ane Ile manurit, gude for corn, girsing and fisching, perteining to M^c^cloyd of the Leozus.

[236. *172.*] Southwart from this Ile lyis ane Ile callit *Ellan Iffurt*, sum manurit land, with gude pasture and scheling of store, with fair hunting of Ottiris out of thair bowris, perteining to M^c^cloyd of the Leozus.

[237. *173.*] Southwart from this Ile lyis ane Ile callit *Scalpay of Haray*, twa mile lang, ane profitable Ile for corn and girsing [and fischinge], perteining to M^c^cloyd of the Haray.

[238. *174.*] Towards the north-eist be 20 mile of sea lyis ane Ile in the sea callit *Fladay*, half mile lang, ane profitable Ile in corn and girsing, and als in fishing, perteining to Donald Gormesoun.

[239. *175.*] Northwart fra this Ile lyis the Ile callit *Ellan Senta,*[103] callit in Inglish the saynt Ile, mair nor twa mile lang, verie profitable for corn, store and fisching, perteining to M^c^cloyd of the Leozus.

On the eist side of this Ile thair is ane Bow made like ane Volt,[104] mair nor ane arrow shot of any man, in manner of ane Volt under earth, throw the quhilk Volt we useit to row or sail with aire[105] boats, for feir of the horrible brak of seais that is on the outwart side of the point quhair that Bow is, but na great schippis may cum thair, perteining to M^c^cloyd of the Leozus.

[240. *176.*] Be eist this lyis ane Ile callit *Senchastell,* callit in Inglish the auld castell, ane strenth full of corn and girsing, and wild fowl nests in it, and als fisching, perteining to M^c^cloyd of the Leozus.

[241. *177.*] Upon the schoir of Loch Briene lyis *Ellan Eu,* half mile lang, full of woods to await upon leill mens geire and gude for theves to the same effect, perteining to M^c^kenzie.

[242. *178.*] Northwart from this Ile lyis *Ellan Gruinord,* mair nor ane mile lang, full of wood, gude for fostering of rebells, perteining to M^c^kenzie.

[243. *179.*] Northwart from this Ile lyis *Ellan na clerach,* half mile lang, gude for girsing and wild fowl eggis, perteining to M^c^kenzie.

[244. *180.*] Narrest this lyis *Ellan af vill,* gude for store and fishing.

[245. *181.*] Narrest this lyis *Havreray moir.*

[246. *182.*] Narrest this lyis *Havreray beg.*

[103] ? Seuta, as in *Buch.*; Senta *BM.*

[104] See Glossary (p. 159).

[105] our *BM.*

[247. *183.*] Besides this lyis *Ellan na neach.*

[248. *184.*] Besides this lyis *Ellan Mertark.*

All thir 8 Iles abovewrittin is in the mouth of Loch bryne.[106]

[249. *207.*] North, or north-west fra this Ile lyis[107] the *Haray* and *Leozus*, quhilk is but ane Ile baith togidder,[108] extending in lenth fra the south-west to the north-eist to 60 miles, and from the north-west to the south-eist 16 mile in breid. Within the south part of this said Ile lyis ane Monasterie with ane steipill, quhilk was foundit and biggit be M^c^cloyd of Haray callit Roadill. This south part of the cuntrie callit Haray is verie fertile and frutfull for corn, store and fisching, and tways mair of delvit nor of teillit land in it. Within this end of the cuntrie thair is ane water with ane gude tak of salmond fische in it, with ane heich grene hill callit Copefeall maist excellent for scheip in these parts, quhairin thair wes (quhan I was thair) scheip without awineris and very auld.[109] In this cuntrie of Haray northwart, betwix it and the Leozus are mony forrests, mony deir[110] but not great of quantitie, verie fair hunting games without any woods, with infinite slauchteris of Otteris and Martrikis. This Ile hes nather wolfis, toddis nor edderis in it. The Leozus is in the north pairt of this Ile, and the maist, also fair and well inhabite at the sea coist, ane fertile

[106] Sentence not in *BM*; Hæ octo proximæ insulæ ante ostium sitæ sunt sinus, quem vulgo lacum Briennum vocant *Buch.* fol. 11.

[107] Now we returne backwards to the Harrey . . . *BM*; Ab his insulis, quæ sinum Briennum præcingunt absunt Haraia & Leogus . . . *Buch.* fol. 11.

[108] Buch. (fol. 11) says: Hæ quidem vnam faciunt insulam, non enim maris infusi æstuarijs, sed limitibus agrorum, & dominorum ditionibus definiuntur (These two divisions form only one island, separated not by the sea, but by the boundaries of the estates and jurisdiction of the chiefs—Aikman's trans.).

[109] *Buch.* (fol. 11) says: Narrat Donaldus Monrous homo doctus, & pius se, cum illic esset, vidisse oues admodum annosas, vtin eo pecoris genere, sine certis dominis vagas (Donald Monro, a pious and well informed man, mentions, that he saw when there, old sheep, old for that species of cattle, wandering about without any particular owner—Aikman's trans.).

frutfull cuntrie, for the maist pairt all beir, with four paroche kirks, and with ane Castell callit Steornvay, with three principall salt water Lochis, verie gude for tak of hering; to wit, Loch Selga farrest to the south-west; Loch Sifort northwart fra that; ane Loch that is lang, and certane small Lochis in it, quhilk is callit the Lochis for the same cause. By this thair are three Lochis not evil for tak of hering; to wit, Loch Steornvay [with] infinite [fresche] water Lochis. In this Leozus thair are 8 waters with great tak of salmond, with 12 waters having ane gude tak of smaller salmonds. In this cuntrie thair is mony scheip, for it is ane verie gude cuntrie for the same: for they ly furth evir on mures and glennis, and enteris nevir in ane house and thair wool is but anes in the zeir clippit aff thame in some fauldis. In this cuntrie all is peitmosland at the sea coist, and the place quhair he wynis his peittis this zeir thair he sawis his beir the next zeir: eftir that he gudes it weill with sea wair. Ane great tak of quhaillis is ofttimes in this cuntrie, swa that be relation of the maist ancient in the cuntrie thair come [26 or] 27 quhaillis young and auld to the teind anes thair. Thair is ane Cove in this cuntrie, quhairin the sea fillis and is twa faddom deip at ebb sea, and four faddom and mair at full sea. Within this Cove thair uses quhyles to be slane with hwikis verie mony haddokis and quhyttingis by men with thair wandis sittand on the craigis of that Cove and Laddes and lasses and women also. Thair is verie mony halk nestis in Leozus and Haray.

[250. *208*.] Towards the north-eist or north north-eist from Leozus 60 miles of sea lyis ane little Ile callit *Ronay*, laich mane land, inhabite and manurit be simple people scant of ony Religion. This Ile is half mile lang, half mile braid: abundand of corn growis in it be delving, abundante of naturall[111] claver girs for scheip. Thair is ane certane

[110] aboundance of deire *BM*.
[111] 'naturall' in *B*, not *M*.

number of ky and scheip ordanet for this Ile be thair awin auld rycht, extending to sa mony as may be sufficient upon the said girsing; and the cuntrie is sa fertile of girsing, that the superexcrescens of the said ky and scheip baith feidis thame in flesche and als payis thair dewties with the same for the maist pairt. Within this Ile thair is sic fair quhyte beir meill maid like flowir, and quhan thay slay thair scheip [they slay them] belly flauchts and stuffis the said skynnis fresche of the beir meill. They send thair dewtie aftirwart to M^c^cloyd of Leozus, with certane reistit muttonnis, and mony reistit wild fowls. Within this Ile thair is ane chapell callit St Ronans chapell, into the quhilk chapell (as the ancients of that cuntrie alledgis) thay use to leave ane spaid and ane schoole quhan ony deid, and upon the morn findis the place of the grave taiknit with ane spaid (as thai alledge). In this Ile thay use to tak mony quhaillis and utheris great fisches.

[251. *209.*] Be sixteen mile of sea towards the west of this Ile lyis ane Ile callit *Swilskeray*, ane mile lang, without girs or hedder, with heich blak craigis and blak fog upon pairt of thame. This Ile is full of wild fowls, and quhan the fowls hes thair birds ripe, men out of the parochin of Niss in Leozus uses to saill thair and tarry thair 7 or 8 dayis and to fetche with thame hame thair boatfull of dry wild fowls with wild fowl fedderis. In this Ile thair hantis ane fowl callit the Colk, little les nor ane goose, quha cummis in vair to the land to [lay] his [112] eggis and to cleck his birdis quhill he [112] bring thame to perfection, and at that time his fleiss of fedderis fallis off him all haillelie, and he flasses [113] to the mayne sea again, and cummis nevir to land quhill the zeiris end again, and than he cummis with his new fleiss of fedderis. This fleiss that he leaves zeirlie upon his nest hes na banes in the fedderis nor any kind of hard thing in thame that may be felt or graipit but uttir fine downis.

[112] her, she *BM* (throughout paragraph).
[113] sayles *BM.*

NOTE ON THE GENEALOGIES

DONALD MONRO'S ' Geneologies of the Cheiff Clans of the Iles ' is worth a closer examination than it may seem to merit at first glance. It gives the descent of the five main branches of the Clan Donald as they existed in his day—Sleat, Islay and Kintyre, Clanranald and Glengarry, Clanian of Ardnamurchan, and the Lochaber Macdonalds. The first step towards appreciating Monro's contribution to our knowledge of Highland genealogy is to construct a family tree based on his manuscript; this will be found opposite page 146, with some additions taken mainly from Donald Gregory's *History of the Western Highlands and Islands* (1836), and the monumental work on *The Clan Donald* (3 vols., 1896-1904), by the Revs. Angus and Archibald Macdonald.

Monro's statements are given more weight by the fact that he was related by marriage to several of the branches of whom he treats. One of his uncles had been married to Margaret, daughter of Alexander of Glengarry by a daughter of Alexander of Lochalsh; while another married Margaret, daughter of Archibald ' the Clerk ' (Captain of the Clanhuistean, or Macdonalds of Sleat). He himself once guided the pen for John Moydertach, Captain of Clanranald, and it is worth remembering that another uncle (Donald, Provost of the Collegiate Church of Tain, and full brother of his father) had done the same for ' Donald Ilis of Sleite ' when that chief signed a bond in 1527, and for Angus, son of Alexander of Glengarry, in 1546.

Regarding the date of Monro's manuscript, it may well have been, like the *Description*, a product of the tour of 1549. From internal evidence, it seems to have been compiled after Donald Gormeson's succession as a child in 1539 (*Clan Donald*, iii 469), and before the death of Sir James Macdonald of Kintyre, which took place in Ireland in 1565, had become known (*Clan Donald*, iii 378).

The order in which Monro places the various branches probably reflects their relative importance in his own day. With the death of Donald Dubh following his rebellion in 1545 (in which nearly all the branches of the family supported him), Sleat became the most powerful, and Donald Gormeson's widespread possessions will be noted in the *Description*; the family of Islay and Kintyre, whose chief appeared in the role of heir to the House of the Isles after the death of Donald Dubh, had not yet suffered eclipse; Clanranald came next, in the person of their Captain, John Moydertach, with (strangely enough, in view of the relationship) no mention of Glengarry; the Macians of Ardnamurchan, descended from a branch which had struck off the main stem in an earlier generation, had not yet disappeared as a territorial family; and last came the Lochaber (or Keppoch) branch, of which Monro mentions no contemporary head, for Ranald McDonald Glasse was beheaded in 1547 after being involved in Lennox's rebellion.

Where it can be checked from other sources, including the records of that time, the manuscript has proved reliable; the few respects in which it differs from other authorities are pointed out in the ' tree ' and in the notes. Gregory quoted Monro on the descent of the Sleat family, and for the pedigree of the Clanian of Ardnamurchan (of which only meagre details can be found elsewhere) Monro is one of the two principal sources of information.

Dr W. Forbes Skene, although admitting that he ' never had access ' to Monro's manuscript, described it as ' most inaccurately printed '. Certainly the previous editions, and the transcripts on which they are based, leave much to be desired; even after being checked with the three existing manuscript variations, the text which follows is probably not exactly as Monro left it. The sources are discussed elsewhere (pp. 148-50), but it should be repeated that for the *Genealogies* (unlike the *Description*) the Sibbald MS. is very cramped and difficult to decipher. The Balfour MS., checked with that of Macfarlane, has therefore been chiefly relied on, and variations between the three MSS. are pointed out in the notes.

HEIR FOLLOWIS THE GENEOLOGIES OF THE CHEIFF CLANS OF THE ILES

COLLECTED BY ME

Sr DONALD MONRO HEIGHE DEANE OF THE ILES

IMPRIMIS *Clandonald*, and of them 5 branches in the Iles, by branches smaller.

First *Donald Gormesone* his kin are called of surname Hutfcheon that is to say the successione of *Hutfcheon McDonald* quhom of they descendit and sprange. Therfor this man is called *Donald Mcdonald Gorme* Vic *Donald Gurmache*, Vic *donald Gorvaiche*, Vic *Hutfcheon* quho wes sone to *Alexander* of *Ila* Earle of Rosse, and Lord of the Iles ore as the heighland men calls him king of the Iles.

And this *Alexander* wes sone to *Donald Earle of Rosse* by the marriage of Valter Lesley Earle of Rosse daughter and heire and this Earle Donald wes the first Earle of memorey that of the *Clandonald*[1] iustly brukit Rosse.

And this *Donald* wes the stock quherfra Clandonald[1] wer named last in ther names quha wes sone to *Ihone* of *Ila* ane of the best that came of that sorte, quho had the *Stewarte* to his vyffe mother to this donald forsaid.

This *Ihone* of *Ila* wes sone to *Angus McAngus*, Vic *Donald* fra quhome they wer called first and of the aulde *Clandonald.*

This Donald wes the sone of *Ragnald McSomerle* (i) [2] Somerledi, fra quhome they wer for a quhyle named and called *Clansomerle.*

[1] Clanronald *M* (see explanation of contractions at p. 44).

[2] This symbol is inserted in all three MSS. between Gaelic names and their Latin equivalents (*cf.* John Elder's letter to Henry VIII, quoted Skene iii 331-2, from Iona Club p. 27, and Irish MSS. quoted Skene iii 462-5, 466-7).

This *Somerle* wes the sone of *Gillebryde McgilleAdam* name Vic *Sella* Vic *Mearghaighe*,[3] Vic *Swyffine*, Vic *Malghwssa*, Vic *Racime*,[4] Vic *Gothofreid* fra quhom they wer called at that tyme *Clan Gothofreid*, that is Clangotheray in hybers Leid, and they wer werey grate men in that tymes of zeire: and ay one called *Clangotherey* quhill Donald gorme quhome I last made mentione.

This [5] *Gotheray* was the sone of *Fergus McEricke*, Vic *Carlayne*,[6] Vic *Ethoy*, Vic *Thola Craisme*, Vic *Ethoy* dewiff Leist (i) Ethodius Vic *Frathriquerwy* (i) fratherus, Vic *Clarpra Lisse Chuyr* (i) Corbredus Vic *Chormweil alada* (i) Cormacus Vic *Airt Lormeche King of Irland*, maist royall in all his actions, Vic *Chwyn chedchahoy* (i) Condus Centibellus King of Irland a royall prince ane lyone lyke in all his actiones of warre of quhome I make ther the stoke in Irland for that he is linially descendit of Gathelus seed.

CLAN EANMORE

The Second Housse of the Clandonald

Sr James Maconeill of kintyre is the second housse of the Iles quho is the sone of *Alexander McIhone* Vic *Anald* (i) Agnaldi,[7] Vic *Ean* (i) Iohanis Vic *Donald Ballay* Vic *Ean* of quhome they are called to surname *Sleight Ean-moire* (i) successio Iohanis Magni, quho wes sone to *Iohne*, the best Lord of the Iles as I have said offe befor quho had the Stewarts doughter to his Ladey, heir I impe this branche to the tree justly as is afforsaid.

CLAN RAGNALD

The Thrid Housse of the Clandonald

Ihone Moydeortreiche is the sone of *Alexander McAllane* (i) filius Alani, Vic *Rorey* (i) Rodorici, Vic *Ean* (i) Iohanis Vic

[3] Mearhaighe *M*. [4] Thus in all MSS. 'Eacime' in previous editions.
[5] Not in *M*. [6] ? Carkyne *B*; Cartayne *S*.
[7] Thus in all MSS. See note on p. 146.

Ragnald (i) Riginaldi quhome I impe to this good *Iohne* of *Ila* his father forsaid, heir sproutit tua branches out of the tree, at once that is the *Clan-ean-moire* and the *Clan-ragnald.*

CLAN-EAN OF ARDNAMORACHIN

The Fourte Housse of the Clandonald

Alexander M^c^donald (i) donaldi *M^c^Ean* [8] (i) Iohanis *M^c^Aloir* (i) Alexandri, *M^c^Angus, M^c^Ean Achechlerwache,*[9] *M^c^Angus moire* quho wes the Lord of the Iles and him I impe to the tree.

ALEXANDER CARRATH

The Fyfte Housse of the Clan-Donald

Neirest this descendit from the housse of *Clan-donald* is *Alexander Carrath,* that is Shawit Alexander, sua that be the countries custome, because heighland [10] men called the fairest hared man Chewit Man, and the chewit the hared and sua furthe, for this *Alexander* wes the fairest hared man (as they say) of aney that ever was, and this said [11] *Alexander* wes brother to this *Donald* of the Iles forsaid and to *Ihone moire* fra quhome *James* of kintyre discendit, and brother of the father syde to *Ragnald* of quhome came the *Clan-ranald.* And this *Carrath* hes maney come of him and good succession in *Locheaber* called *Clan-ranald M^c^donald-Glasse* Vic *Alexander* quhilk bruikes a pairt of Locheaber sinsyne.

There wes by thir I have wrettin offe, *Iohne, Gothofred* and *Angus,* the quhilks had nae successione.

FINIS

8 Eean *B.*
9 Perhaps an adjectival form.
10 the Heighland *M.*
11 this Alexander *M.*

APPENDIX I

THE COUNCIL OF THE ISLES

DONALD MONRO's notice of the Council of the Lords of the Isles, which used to meet on a small island in Loch Finlaggan, in Islay, is at once the earliest and the most detailed of the three now available.[1] As it is missing from the manuscripts on which all previous editions of Monro's *Description* are based, and is now published for the first time, it is appropriate that what is known about the meetings, members and functions of this unique body should be examined.

In Loch Finlaggan today, the crumbling ruins of the great MacDonald's 'palace work' still bear witness to the vanished glory of the Lords of the Isles. The whole site is plainly on a more elaborate scale than anything to be seen at their other castles, such as Ardtornish and Aros on the Sound of Mull; and, as the centre of the old Gaelic principality, it is to be hoped that it may yet be systematically examined, and what remains of its buildings preserved from further decay.[2] Meantime,

[1] See pages 56-7. The other two accounts are in the 'History of the Macdonalds', attributed to Hugh Macdonald, a Skye seneachie, and said to have been written in the reign of Charles II, certainly after Jan. 1627/28 (printed in *H.P.*, i 23-5 ; Iona Club, 297 ; *O.P.S.*, ii (i) 267) ; and in Martin (written about 1695), 272-3.

[2] David N. Mackay, in his *Clan Warfare* (1922), p. 54 note, and Miss I. F. Grant, LL.D., in her Rhind Lectures of 1950, called for the study and preservation of the ruins (*The Scotsman*, 24 Oct. 1950), but so far nothing has been done. Finds have been made here in the past : a carved stone, found 'under the ruins' about 1830, is illustrated in J. F. Campbell's *Popular Tales of the West Highlands* (1862), iv 400 ; and a Roman coin belonging to the fourth year of Diocletian (A.D. 287-288), sent to Sir George Macdonald for inspection about 1918, was stated to have been found 'on an island in Fin Laggan Loch, Islay' (*P.S.A.S.*, lii 250). On a grassy plain to the north of the ruins, said to have been a garden, it has been suggested that the magnates joined the people in the 'mazy dance'—a conception not out of keeping with the Macdonald seneachie's statement quoted at p. 106 (Graham, 28 ; *Islay* (1850), 19, (1878), 21 ; *H.P.*, i 24).

we must rest content with noting what is to be seen there today.

Eilean Mòr, now almost joined to the shore near the north-west corner of the loch, is so overgrown with matted grass and nettles that little but the outlines of its buildings can be distinguished without excavation. In 1868, a visitor reported that 'to judge from the remains, the castle must have been of considerable extent', and his sketch bears this out; when the place was surveyed ten years later, the site of an elaborate series of buildings was recorded; and 'traces of the keep and of an outer wall broken at intervals by round towers' are mentioned in 1895 by Graham in his *Carved Stones of Islay*.[3] Nearby are the ruins of the chapel dedicated to St Finlaggan (a contemporary of Columba), which was anciently in the patronage of the Lords of the Isles.[4] It was one of those roofed in during the 14th century by the 'good John of Isla', who also gave 'the proper furniture for the service of God' and maintenance for the officiating clergy.[5] There was a burial ground to the south of the chapel, and several examples of the fine West Highland carved tombstones have been collected within its walls. According to Pennant, the wives and children of the Lords of the Isles were buried on this island, while they themselves had the right of sepulture in Iona; and one of these ladies, as we know, was a Scottish princess. Both Martin and Pennant mention the ruins of a pier and the quarters of MacDonald's guards on the shores of Loch Finlaggan, and all over Islay there are reminders of their rule.[6]

[3] 'Gowrie', 260, and sketch opp. 261 ; C. MacLagan in Stirling Nat. Hist. and Arch. Soc. (1883), 37-8 ; O.S. map, scale 1 : 2500, sheet cxcviii 5 ; Graham, 28.

[4] *R.P.S.*, i 134 (911).

[5] 'The Book of Clanranald', in Skene, iii 402 ; *Rel. Celt.*, ii 159, 161 ; and Scott, note to canto i.

[6] Graham, 28. Martin, 273. Pennant, i 260. Anderson, 358. At Ballygrant, 'townland of corn', near Finlaggan I was told that the Lords had their stores of grain, although no specific site was named ; at Emeraconart,

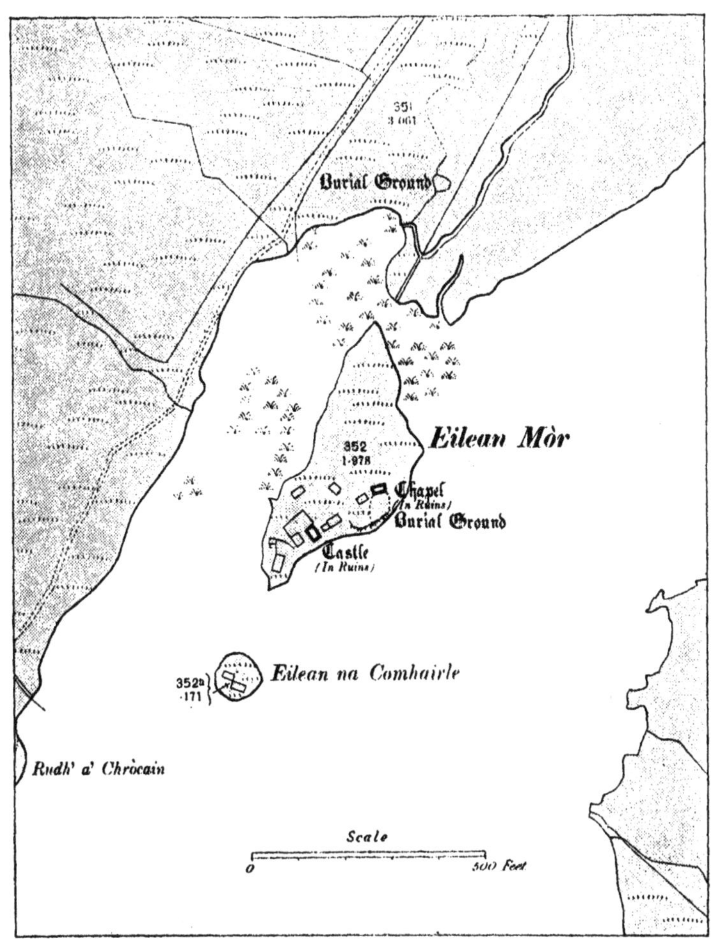

Part of Loch Finlaggan in Islay, showing the Council Isle (*Eilean na Comhairle*)

Beyond Eilean Mòr, and some fifty yards to the south of it, lies the Council Isle itself, still known as *Eilean na Comhairle.* A boat is now required to reach it, but a line of boulders in the shallower part of the dividing channel, next the larger island, shows where a causeway or stepping-stones may once have joined them. Rising in the centre to some twelve or fifteen feet above the level of the loch, the islet is only about ninety yards round, and one-sixth of an acre in extent. Except on the narrow beach encircling it, the surface is thickly covered with reed grass and wild flowers—buttercup, yellow vetch and meadow-sweet, willow-herb, hemlock and sneezewort, ragwort, knapweed and mint. Pushing one's way through the tall grass—over four feet high—across the top of the island, one can feel large stones underfoot. These seem to lie in the position of the two rectangular sites marked on the Ordnance Survey map; perhaps they mark the foundations of the ' counsell-house ', of which we now learn for the first time from Monro's detailed account of Finlaggan and the Council Isle. It had always been assumed, before this came to light, that the Council met in the open air.[7]

about two miles southwest, Pennant (i 252) recorded ' the vestiges of some buts where the great *Macdonald* exercised his men at archery ' ; near the head of Lochindaal is *Tràigh Longa,* ' shore of the ships ', with a line of stones running out into the loch where Pennant was told that Macdonald had a harbour for his galleys (i 253-4, and *Islay* (1900), 105) ; Ballinaby, on the way to Kilchoman on the west coast, was the property of the MacBeaths or Beatons, chief Physicians of the Isles (*Hist. MSS.*, iv app. 480, 471) ; and at Kilchoman itself, on the site of the manse and garden, the Macdonalds are said to have had a residence and a glen where they kept their cattle (*H.P.*, i 33 ; Pennant, i 254). ' Near to Kilchoman, I observed an old, ruinous gloomy building, which was once the seat of the turbulent Macdonald, prince of the Isles, but it is now peacefully inhabited by the minister of the parish ' (R. Jameson, *Mineralogy of the Scottish Isles* (Edin. 1800), i 162).

[7] One of the illustrations in McIan, i part xi, shows the Lord of the Isles, clad in shirt of mail, and having his skull-cap adorned with eagle's wing and heather badge, ' sitting in judgment on the Tom Moid, or law hill, in Eillean Comheurlich, with his barons around him ' ; it is reproduced wholly or in part in C. Fraser-Mackintosh, *The Last Macdonalds of Isla* (1895), 23 ; *The Celtic Monthly*, vii (1899), 95 ; and Mackenzie (1906), opp. 80. A novelist's

The setting, at the head of a loch in a long sloping valley, bears a striking resemblance to the site of the old Shetland Law Ting, which, in Monro's time, still sat on a holm in Tingwall Loch.[8] But anyone familiar with the rugged grandeur of Thingvellir in Iceland, or with the Tynwald Hill in the Isle of Man, will look in vain at Finlaggan or Tingwall for any parallel with these other historic centres of the old Viking world.[9] How the Scottish sites, which can hardly have been selected with defence in view, served their purpose is puzzling. In both places, however, the object

impression of the scene is in Evan John [Simpson], *Crippled Splendour* (1938), 449-54. *Islay* (1959) says of the Council Isle (N(4)19): 'There is no causeway to the castle island apparent, nor any evidence (such as traces of logs under water, or stone arrangements) to show it as a crannog. On the isle are remains of buildings. Three small pieces of broken flint (not common here) were found on the verges of this islet.' There is a tradition that Eilean Mhuireill farther down Loch Finlaggan was used for MacDonald's prisoners (ditto, N(4)20).

[8] Ancient Monts., 12th report, iii 124 (1522). Although 'transferred by later antiquaries from the holm to the mainland' (Burton, *Ultima Thule* (1875), ii 197), the traditional site is accepted by most writers on Shetland (*e.g.* Brand, Gifford, *Old Stat. Acc.*, Edmonston, Sir Walter Scott, Hibbert, Cowie and Tudor); the election of Nicol Reid of Aith to the office of Lawman-General of all Zetland was dated 'In the Ting holm of Tingwall' on 27 July 1532 (*Oppressions of the Sixteenth Century in the Islands of Orkney and Zetland* (Edin. 1859), 36-7; Gilbert Goudie, *The Celtic and Scandinavian Antiquities of Shetland* (1904), 93, 146, 230). But Professor Einar Ol. Sveinsson of the University of Iceland, does not see how the Shetland Althing could be held on this small holm, now a peninsula, where he addressed the first Viking Congress on 9 July 1950.

[9] It used to be thought that the Icelandic Althing met on a sort of island in the plain named Spöngin, a narrow strip of land bounded by two deep water-filled chasms, Flosagjá and Nikulásgjá (Dufferin, *Letters from High Latitudes* (1857 edn.), 94-6; G. W. Dasent, *The Story of Burnt Njal* (Edin. 1861), vol. i, intro. pp. cxxviii-ix, and plan at p. cxxx; Burton, *op. cit.*, ii 197-8). Later researches, however, have placed the central features of the Althing—the Lögberg and Lögrettá—on the eastern edge of the great Almannagjá, overlooking the plain (Eirikr Magnusson, note in Wm. Morris's *Collected Works*, viii (1911) 242; Matthias Thordarson, *The Althing, Iceland's Thousand Year Old Parliament*, (Reykjavík 1930), 9, and *Thingvöllur: Althingisstadurinn Forni* (Reykjavík 1945), *passim* and map; Kristján Eldjárn, *Brief Notes on Thingvellir* (1953), with photoplan); and it was there that the millenary celebrations were held in 1930. For the Manx Tynwald, see Cubbon, 103-9.

may have been to ensure that, although the councillors could not be interrupted, justice would be dispensed within the sight of all. Even here, however, we are faced with a contradiction, if the Council sat in a building—unless, as in the Isle of Man, its only covering was a canopy overhead.

(i)

A subordinate body termed *Principes Insularum*, the Princes or Chiefs of the Isles, is mentioned frequently during the entire duration of the Norse Kingdom of the Isles, which came to an end in 1266. Their recognition of the authority of the King of the Isles, says Skene in his *Celtic Scotland*, was necessary to his assumption of that position. 'We see them electing a king and occasionally deposing a king; and that this body consisted of persons partly of Norwegian and partly of Gaelic descent is evident, from their sometimes deferring to the authority of the king of Norway, and at other times appealing to Ireland for aid. . . .'[10] Islay is reputed to have been, next to Man itself, the favourite seat of the Norse kings of the Isles: and Godred Crovan, who effected the political union of Man and the Hebrides, died in Islay about 1095.[11]

A Gaelic account of the earliest known meeting of the island chiefs, after they had become subject to the Scottish Crown, seems to place it in the Isle of Eigg, and not in Islay, although the wording is obscure. When John Lord of the Isles died, probably in 1386, the succession passed to the eldest son by his second wife, who was a daughter of King Robert II. In the *Book of Clanranald*, compiled by the MacVurich seneachies, we are told that Ranald (John's eldest son by his first marriage), who was 'high steward' at the time of his father's death, 'called a meeting of the

[10] Munch, i 54, 56, 64, 68. Skene, iii 37. Cubbon, 79, 80.
[11] Henderson, 194, quoting Camden. Munch, i 144.

nobles of the Isles and his brethren to one place, and gave the staff of lordship to his brother at Kildonan in Eigg, and he was nominated MacDomnall and Donald of Isla, contrary to the opinion of the men of the Isles '.[12]

The accounts of the Council of the Isles by Monro, Macdonald and Martin were all written after the fall of the Lordship in 1493. It will be useful, therefore, to check and supplement them by reference to the actual charters granted by the Lords of the Isles. Ten of those which have survived, either in the original or through later confirmations by the Crown, contain explicit reference to the Council, all but one of them dated during the reign of John, the last Lord of the Isles, who succeeded in 1449. They record grants made at Inverness in 1444, at Dingwall in 1463 and 1464, at Ayremore (? in Knapdale) and again twice at Dingwall in 1467, at Aros in Mull in 1469, and at Oronsay in 1492. From these places the Lord of the Isles issued charters '*de assensu et consensu et matura deliberatione* (*totius*) *concilii sui*', or according to an almost identical form of words.[13]

It is disconcerting, at first sight, to find no record from these days of the Council having met at Finlaggan; but that is not to say that Monro, Macdonald and Martin exaggerated its importance. Islay would be the headquarters of the principality of the Isles, except for the period (*c.* 1429-1475) when, being also Earl of Ross with large estates on the mainland, the Lord of the Isles had his courts at the castle of Dingwall or at Inverness. He did in fact grant charters '*apud Insulam S. Finlagani in Yle*' in 1427, at Finlaggan again in 1432, and '*apud Ila*' in 1476 and 1479. The well-known Gaelic charter of Islay lands granted in 1408—sole

[12] Skene, iii 403. *Rel. Celt.*, ii 161. Norman Macpherson in *P.S.A.S.*, xii, 579.

[13] For details see note I: Charters of the Lords of the Isles (p. 139).

survivor of those written in that language—may also have been signed at Finlaggan.[14]

(ii)

No record remains to show whether the members of the Council were appointed by the Lord of the Isles himself, or by his principal subjects. A manuscript in the British Museum has been quoted for the statement that 'the chiefs of the Yles chose a king, and adjoined to him ane counsel of the wisest'.[15]

Regarding the composition of the Council, our authorities enter into some detail:—

MONRO: In this Ile thair conveinit 14 of the Iles best Barons, that is to say, four greatest of the Nobles callit Lords; to wit M^c^gillane of Doward, M^c^gillane of Lochbuy, M^c^cloyde of Haray, & M^c^cloyde of Leozus.[16] Thir four Barons forsaid might be callit Lords, & were haldin as Lords at sic time. Four Thanes[17] of les living & estate; to wit, M^c^ginnihin,[18] M^c^naic,[19] M^c^neill of Gighay & M^c^neill of Barray. Uther four great men of living of thair royall blude of Clan-donald lineally descendit; to wit Clan-donald of Kintyre, M^c^ane of Ardnanmirquhame Clan-Ronald, & Clan-Alister Carryche in Lochaber; with the Bishop & the Abbot of Icolmkill.

MACDONALD: Macdonald had his council at Island Finlaggan, in Isla, to the number of sixteen, viz.:—four Thanes, four Armins,

[14] For details see note I. *R.M.S.*, ii 485 (2287). Sir William Fraser, *Earls of Cromartie*, ii 511. *Clan Donald*, i 557-9; *R.M.S.*, ii 259 (1277). *R.M.S.*, ii 301 (1449); *Nat. MSS.*, ii 46; *Islay* (1895), 16-17; *Clan Donald*, i 513-15. *Invernessiana*, 184. It has been suggested that Richard II, after losing the English throne, found his way to the court of the Lord of the Isles at Finlaggan (Tytler, ii 97-8; *Clan Donald*, i 142-3; D. N. Mackay, 54 note), but the person referred to by Bower and Wyntoun was more probably an impostor (John Riddell, *Tracts, Legal and Historical* (Edin. 1835), 59-60; E. W. M. Balfour-Melville, *James I, King of Scots* (London 1936), 23).

[15] 'Manner of choosing the Kings of Scotland of old', MS. in British Museum (not located), quoted Logan, i 193-4.

[16] Maclean of Duart, Maclean of Lochbuie, Macleod of Harris, and Macleod of Lewis.

[17] 'The Lords of the Isles created thanes and sub-thanes at pleasure' ('History of the Macdonalds' in *H.P.*, i 27).

[18] Mackinnon.

[19] Unidentified. 'Macknaie' in Sibbald's own MS. 'Description'.

that is to say, Lords or sub-Thanes, four Bastards, (i.e.) Squires, or men of competent estates, who could not come up with Armins or Thanes; [and four [20]] that is, freeholders, or men that had their lands in factory, as Macgee of the Rinds of Isla, MacNicoll in Portree in Sky, and MacEachern, Mackay, and MacGillevray in Mull, Macillemhaoel or MacMillan, etc.

MARTIN: The High Court of Judicature, consisting of fourteen, sat always here.

It will be noticed that the two earliest accounts agree that the Council included four representatives of each of the ranks or grades to which they refer, and of this there is a likely explanation. The Lordship of the Isles was a confederacy made up of a number of semi-independent clans under their own chiefs, and the great MacDonald himself was picturesquely known as *Buachaille nan Eileanan*, the Shepherd or Herdsman of the Isles.[21] The anonymous description of the Hebrides, almost contemporary with Monro's, states that the 'whole Isles of Scotland' were formerly divided into four parts, based respectively on the four large islands of Lewis, Skye, Mull and Islay.[22] These

[20] 'The Gaelic word expressive of the men who held their lands in factory is evidently omitted' (Iona Club, 326).

[21] *Clan Traditions and Popular Tales of the Western Highlands and Islands* (London, 1895), coll. Rev. John Gregorson Campbell, pp. 67-8, 86, in 'Waifs and Strays of Celtic Tradition' series. I. F. Grant, *The Clan Donald* (1952), 13.

[22] 'The haill Iles of Scotland were devidit in four pairts of auld, viz. Lewis, Sky, Mule and Yla, and the remanent haill Iles were reknit but as pertinents and pendicles of the said four Iles, and were devidit amangis thir four Iles, and annext thairto in this manner. First to the Ile of Lewis wes annext the Iles of Wist, Barra, Harrayis, Ronalewis, Pabla in Harreik, Helsker, Collismown and Iit [later 'Irt', St Kilda]. To the Ile of Sky were annext Raarsa, Eg, Romb, Canna, Ellan na muck and Scalpa. Perteining to the Ile of Mule were Lismoir, Tuahannais [later 'the twa Iles callit the Hwnayis'], Ulloway, Commatra, Inschennycht, Sanct Colmisinche, alias Colmkill, Tireich and Coll. And to the fourth Ile of Yla was conjoynit the Iles of Dewra alias Iura, Collonsa, Geiga, Rauchlyne, Seillonyng [later listed as two isles], Scarba. . . . Thair is also ane Ness passand south-west fra the lands of Ardmwrche, quhilk Ness is callit Romwrche [Ardnamurchan Point] and divides thir haill Iles in twa; viz. in south and north Iles, viz. the Iles of Ila and Mule with thair saids pertinents, lyand fra the said Ness to the south, and the Iles of Lewis and Sky to the north.' (Skene, iii 428, checked with Thomas-Skene MS., p. 22).

divisions correspond almost exactly—Skye having taken the place of Uist—with the four great baronies created by Alexander III after the cession of the Isles to him in 1266.[23] Probably Norse in origin, they would form a natural basis on which to constitute the Council of the Isles, which does not appear on record until the whole territory had been consolidated under the sway of the Lord of the Isles in the 15th century.[24] Changes in ownership would no doubt vary the membership, but the basic structure remained.[25]

No complete list of the councillors present at any one meeting has survived, but it will be useful to examine the names of the witnesses who attested the decisions of the Council as a whole.[26] At one time or another, they include all but four of the fourteen mentioned by Monro, although their patronymic styles are not always easy to identify. ' M^c^naie ' is either missing or hiding behind another name, and Clanranald, Macneil of Barra, and the Bishop of the Isles do not figure in any of the lists; but the last two witnessed other charters granted personally by the Lord of the Isles.[27] In addition, we find four other chiefs from

[23] See endpaper maps. The four great Barons were the Earl of Ross, who was given Skye and Lewis ; Angus Macdonald of Islay ; Allan MacRuari of Garmoran and the North Isles, who obtained Uist, Barra, Eigg and Rum ; and John (Ewin) de Ergadia, the lord of Lorne, who had Mull, Jura, Coll and Tiree. See Gregory, 22-8, 32, 36 ; MacLeod, 26, 74, 76.

[24] For reference to the four administrative groups as a survival from the Norse regime and the basis of the Hebridean participation in the medieval Tynwald assemblies in the Isle of Man, see Megaw, 57-62 ; Kinvig, 50-3, 65-6, and Cubbon, 82-90. For a Bull of Pope Gregory IX, dated 30 July 1231 and preserved in a very imperfect form, enumerating the possessions of the Bishop of Sodor, see *S.H.R.*, viii 258-63, and Cubbon, 86, 155.

[25] ' But now [*c.* 1577-82] thir Iles are becum under sundrie mens dominions, quhairthrow thai answer not to the saids principall Iles, zit thai keip the lawis and uses of the samine for the maist pairt, and speciallie of thair zeirlie dewteis, as heireftir shall be declairit. Be thir Iles foirsaids thair is mony small Ilands and Inches in Scotland, quhairof the names are not publist, nor zit in reputation, but worthie of habitation or descryving, quhairthrow we omitt the saymn quhill thai be bettir inhabite and esteimit of.' (Skene, iii 428, and MS.)

[26] See note I : Charters of the Lords of the Isles (p. 139).

[27] *R.M.S.*, ii 479 (2264), 485 (2287).

the western isles and coasts—namely Maclean of Coll, Maclean of Ardgour, MacQuarrie of Ulva, and MacDuffie of Colonsay. It will be observed that, while some of the members have a territorial qualification, others have a place because of their blood relationship with the great MacDonald: Donald Balloch, Lord of Dunivaig and the Glens and head of the Kintyre branch, who was present at three meetings and represented by his son and heir at a fourth, is named first among the witnesses on these occasions, and he is described in a deed of 1475 as '*primus et principalis conciliarus*' of John Lord of the Isles.[28]

When the Council met at Dingwall or Inverness, we find Munro of Foulis, representative of the Earl of Ross in that part, and other mainland lords in attendance on their feudal superior. There too, however, we find also among the witnesses island chiefs like Donald Balloch, Maclean of Duart, Lochbuie and Coll, Macneil of Gigha, Mackinnon of Mishnish, MacQuarrie of Ulva, and MacDuffie of Colonsay, who thus seem to have had a place in the Council even when it met in the heart of the Earldom of Ross. It is hard to identify any of the lesser members named by Macdonald as having 'had their lands in factory', but they may have been among the '*plures alii*' who remain unnamed at the end of more than one charter.[29]

(iii)

In considering the powers and functions of the Council, as well as on general historical grounds, we must deplore the loss of the records of the Isles, which have vanished as surely as their keepers have disappeared as Lords of Colonsay. We are left, therefore, to glean what we can from other

[28] MS. 'Macdonald Collections', ii 1193. *Clan Donald*, i 548.

[29] See *e.g.* charter of 11 Feb. 1443/4 (MS. 'Macdonald Collections', ii 111; *Clan Donald*, i 533-4). A statement such as 'seldom if ever was there a Council of the Lord of the Isles which did not include a Nicolson' (J. G. Nicolson, *The Clan Nicolson*, 32) is apparently no more than a guess.

sources about the Highland councils where—as Macaulay put it—'men who would not have been qualified for the duty of parish clerks sometimes argued questions of peace and war, of tribute and homage, with ability worthy of Halifax and Caermarthen '.[30]

Although Monro makes no mention of it, it is fairly certain that the Council would play an important part in the ceremony of inaugurating the Lords of the Isles. Here is what our other two authorities have to say on the subject:—

MACDONALD : I thought fit to annex the ceremony of proclaiming the Lord of the Isles. At this the Bishop of Argyle, the Bishop of the Isles, and seven priests, were sometimes present ; but a bishop was always present, with the chieftains of all the principal families, and a *Ruler of the Isles.* There was a square stone, seven or eight feet long, and the tract of a man's foot cut thereon, upon which he stood, denoting that he should walk in the footsteps and uprightness of his predecessors, and that he was installed by right in his possessions. He was clothed in a white habit, to shew his innocence and integrity of heart, that he would be a light to his people, and maintain the true religion. The white apparel did afterwards belong to the poet by right. Then he was to receive a white rod in his hand, intimating that he had power to rule, not with tyranny and partiality, but with discretion and sincerity. Then he received his forefathers' sword, or some other sword, signifying that his duty was to protect and defend them from the incursions of their enemies in peace or war, as the obligations and customs of his predecessors were. The ceremony being over, mass was said after the blessing of the bishop and seven priests, the people pouring their prayer for the success and prosperity of their new created Lord. When they were dismissed, the Lord of the Isles feasted them for a week thereafter; gave liberally to the monks, poets, bards and musicians. You may judge that they spent liberally without any exceptions of persons.

MARTIN : There was a big stone of seven feet square, in which there was a deep impression made to receive the feet of Macdonald ; for he was crowned King of the Isles standing in this stone, and swore that he would continue his vassals in the possession of their lands, and do exact justice to all his subjects : and then his father's sword was put into his hand. The Bishop of Argyll and seven priests annointed him

[30] Mackinnon (1912), 325. Macaulay, *History of England*, chap. xiii.

king, in presence of all the heads of the tribes in the isles and continent, and were his vassals ; at which time the orator rehearsed a catalogue of his ancestors, etc.

There is no evidence that the negotiation of treaties and alliances fell within the province of the Council as a whole, although the Lords of the Isles were several times in league with the King of England and others against the King of Scots. From his castle on the Sound of Mull, in October 1461, the last Lord granted a commission to his cousin Ranald and to Duncan, Archdeacon of the Isles, which resulted in the 'Treaty of Ardtornish' with Edward IV. It was issued in the style of an independent sovereign, as Sir Walter Scott pointed out, but—although members of the Council were at Ardtornish in that month—there is no mention among the papers connected with the treaty of the consent of the Council of the Isles having been sought or obtained.[31]

The Council's decisions, it appears, were concerned rather with domestic affairs within the island principality. Adding the feudal power to their patriarchal authority, the Lords of the Isles granted charters to members of their family, to some of their trusted councillors, and to others within their wide dominions. It is not easy to discern under what circumstances the Council's consent was deemed necessary or desirable; for while their imprimatur supports the grant of Lochalsh and Sleat to the last Lord's brothers Celestine and Hugh, and a charter to Maclean of Lochbuie of the bailliary of Tiree carries the consent and bears the

[31] Rymer, xi 486-7. *Rotuli*, ii 402, 405-7. Scott, canto i note. But *cf.* Gregory, 47, followed by Tytler, ii 191, where the commission is said to be granted 'by the advice of his principal vassals and kinsmen, assembled in council at his castle of Ardtornish'. On 10 Oct. 1461 Donald of Donawag and Glynnys, Lachlan McGilleon of Doward, Celestine of Lochailche, Hugh of Slete, Torquall McLeoid of Leoghas, Torlet Ferchardi of Carna, and Hector son of Torlet witnessed a charter by the Lord of the Isles—in which his Council is not mentioned—at Ardtornish (Original seen at Inveraray Castle, by courtesy of the Duke of Argyll ; abstract in Argyll Inventory, i 431 ; *Hist. MSS.*, iv app. p. 482, no. 161 ; *O.P.S.*, ii (i) 193, 309, 341, 382.

seals of his fellow-councillors, grants of land to Maclean of Duart and Macneil of Barra are issued by the authority of the Lord of the Isles alone.

A delicate question which members of the Council might be called on to decide was that of marriage, even in the ruling family itself. Macdonald tells how Hugh of Sleat 'was bound by his father's will not to marry [a second time] but by the consent of twelve of the principal men of his name and the Heritors of the Isles'. A charter granted at Aros with the consent of the whole Council in 1469, however, names those to be consulted as Donald of Dunivaig and the Glens, Celestine of Lochalsh, Lachlan Maclean of Duart, and Alexander Macian of Ardnamurchan, or their heirs.[32] On another occasion, a marriage agreement between Hector Maclean of Lochbuie on one side and John Ross of Balnagown and his son and heir Alexander on the other was entered into at Dingwall in 1475 with the consent of John Earl of Ross and Lord of the Isles, his daughter Lady Margaret, and his brother Hugh, 'and vtheris gentillis of the saide lordis counsale quhilkis war than for the tyme'.[33]

In matters of law, all are agreed that the Council of the Isles was the supreme court:—

MONRO: Thir 14 persons sat down into the Counsell-Ile, & decernit, decreitit & gave suits furth upon all debaitable matters according to the Laws made be Renald McSomharkle callit in his time King of the Occident Iles, & albeit thair Lord were at his hunting or at ony uther games, zit thai sate every ane at thair Counsell ministring justice. In thair time thair was great peace & welth in the Iles throw the ministration of justice.

MACDONALD: There was a judge in every Isle for the discussion of all controversies, who had lands from Macdonald for their trouble, and likewise the eleventh part of every action decided. But there might be still an appeal to the Council of the Isles. MacFinnon was obliged to see weights and measures adjusted; and MacDuffie, or MacPhie of Colonsay, kept the records of the Isles.

[32] *H.P.*, 59, 97. [33] *Acta Dom. Conc.*, i 346-7. *O.P.S.*, ii (i) 311-12.

MARTIN : The High Court of Judicature, consisting of fourteen, sat always here ; and there was an appeal to them from all the Courts in the isles : the eleventh share of the sum in debate was due to the principal judge.

It is unfortunate that we know nothing of the decrees laid down in the 12th century by the son of Somerled, nor indeed of any Gaelic code of law in Scotland, if any such ever existed. But the people's respect for the law, or fear of it, is shown by the long-preserved traditions of the places where judgment was delivered.[34] In Islay itself, besides the Council Isle, there used to be pointed out a terraced hill of judgment, resembling the Manx Tynwald.[35]

* * *

With the final forfeiture of the Lordship in 1493, the Council of the Isles as such ceased to exist, although most of its members were confirmed in the ownership of their territories by the Crown. Finlaggan appears again as the scene of family conclave, however, for it was there that three

[34] Pennant, i 351. Cameron, 141-2. Just as the Justiciar had his reward, so the local judges or *brieves* held lands from their ruler and received the eleventh part of every subject under dispute ; the office was hereditary in families such as the Morrisons in Lewis, but the people are said to have submitted willingly to their authority and censure (Sir R. Gordon, *A Genealogical History of the Earldom of Sutherland* (Edin. 1813), 268 ; Thomas, 507). 'Ane pairt of this Ile of Sky callit Strathvardeill pertenis to ane Laird callit McKynvin, given to him be McConneill [Macdonald] for to be judge and decide all questionnis and debaitts that happenis to fall betwin pairties throw playing at cairtis or dyce or sic uther pastime' (Thomas-Skene MS., in Skene, iii 432).

[35] MacCulloch (1819), ii 234-5. Anderson, 359. Worsaae, 278. *O.P.S.*, ii (i) 272. MacCulloch, from whom the others seem to copy, mentions no exact site, but he may refer to Dun Nosebridge ('Gowrie', 292-3 ; Graham, 34-5 ; V. Gordon Childe in *P.S.A.S.*, lxix 83). Local tradition pointed to a site near the mouth of the River Laggan, called *Tigh-lagh Chillmacheallaich*, as that where the chief court of appeal in the Hebrides used to meet (*Islay* (1878), 32 ; (1900), 60-1). There is a terraced mound surmounted by a stone tower at the entrance to Islay House, called *Cnoc na Croiche*, Gallows Hill (*Islay* (1850), 7 ; (1878), 18 ; (1900), 67). It has even been suggested that the island took its name from Gaelic *lagh*, law (*Islay* (1850), 3; (1878), 11), but this derivation is not accepted.

leaders of the Clan Donald of Kintyre were made prisoner in 1494 by Macian of Ardnamurchan, later to be hurried off to Edinburgh and hanged on the Burgh Muir.[36] When Donald Dubh, the last male descendant of the Lords of the Isles, raised the standard of rebellion in 1545, he revived the Council on the old model, and chose a rendezvous near Islay for its meeting.[37] Half a century later, too, the chiefs who were summoned to meet the King's Lieutenant at Aros in 1608, and those who signed the 'Statutes of Iona' in the following year, were virtually the same as the members of the Council of the Isles listed by Monro.[37] It has even been claimed that the 'Scots Council of 15 Lords'—the Court of Session, established in 1532 and known as 'the auld fifteen'—was erected in imitation of the Council which used to gather round the Lord of the Isles at Finlaggan.[38]

The table of stone where the Council sat, and the stone on which the Lords of the Isles were inaugurated, were carried away by the Earl of Argyll, probably during his expedition to Islay in 1615.[39] By the end of the century, the houses, chapel and other buildings at Finlaggan had become ruinous.[40] Since then they have steadily been falling into further decay, and the centre of the old Gaelic principality is in danger of being forgotten if something is not done before it is too late.

[36] Skene, iii 405. *Rel. Celt.*, ii 163. Gregory, 89-90.

[37] See note I (p. 144). For 'Ellancarne' see note A (pp. 121-2).

[38] 'Rentale of the Parishes of the Island' (1722), quoted in *Islay* (1895), 533, refers to Buchanan's account of the Council Isle taken from Monro, and adds: 'It is alleged that our Scots Councill of 15 Lords was first erected in imitation of the great McDonald his Councill in the said island'. The judicial complement of the Court of Session was recently raised again to 15 after a lapse of over 120 years (*The Scotsman*, 17 Feb. 1954).

[39] *H.P.*, i 24.

[40] Martin, 273.

APPENDIX II

IDENTIFYING THE ISLANDS

THERE can be few people, even in our own day, who know all the islands from Man to North Rona by personal acquaintance. From internal evidence,[1] we can be sure that Monro wrote from first-hand knowledge about Lewis and Harris, Barra, and probably South Uist and Iona; no doubt he knew many of the other islands also, but for some groups it is plain that he had to rely on second-hand information, knowing them only slightly or from hearsay, and this makes a number of them difficult or impossible to identify. It should be remembered, too, that Monro did not have the accurate maps which we possess to fix in his memory even those islands which he had visited.

I do not claim to have a complete knowledge of the Hebrides, but over a period of years I have visited and stayed in many of them. Where my local knowledge was deficient, I have consulted a wide variety of books and maps, ancient and modern, and applied for information and help from those who knew islands unknown to me. Probably some names which baffled me may yet be recognised by others, and I will welcome any suggestions which readers may be able to offer.

As an example of what persistence and good fortune can do, I may mention the five Small Isles of Jura [48-52] which had not previously been identified in Monro's list. While approaching Craighouse by steamer, I happened to be puzzling over the island given by Sibbald as 'Ellan diamhoin', or 'IdleIle'—Ellan Drauin or Dranin (*Bal.*), Ellan dravin (*Macf.*), Idyle or Iydle iyle; quæ Ociosorum

[1] Introduction, p. 10

dicitur (*Buch.*); Isle of Idlemen (*Buch.M.*); island of the Otiosi (*Buch.* 1690, *Buch.A.*)[2]. The origin of this name is obscure, unless it was given to a place to which those with no occupation were sent; but the only Eilean Diomhain listed in the *West Coast Pilot* is one of the Small Isles of Jura, and once this is realised the other four islands are easily identified.

This group, in Monro's list, is wrongly placed immediately before Lismore. Among others which he gives in a confusing order, perhaps because he did not know them himself, are the islands lying off the coast of Lorne [3] [37-57] and the Lismore group [56-68], both of which would fall within the See of Argyll and not that of the Isles. Dr MacCulloch took Monro's list of islands round Islay as an example of fictitious names, but with the aid of Blaeu's *Atlas* I have identified ten out of Monro's 19.[4] The Barra Isles [156-65] are among others which present several difficulties.[5] There is no certainty that Monro's acquaintance with North Rona and Sulisgeir [250, 251] was first-hand,[6] and he may have obtained his information about them from the men of Ness in Lewis or from MacLeod's factor.

Changes in name which have occurred during the past four centuries may well be responsible for some of our difficulties, for the old names are not all so well known as that of St Kilda [Hirta, 184]. Monro's 'Ellan na muk' [98], off the eastern coast of Oronsay, is now called Eilean Ghaoidmeal, Gartmeal or Ghurdmail.[7] Scarpnamult [162] near Barra is now Maol Domhnaich, Island of the tonsured one of the Lord—a remarkable instance of a name being

[2] These contractions refer to the various MSS. of Monro and the editions of Buchanan (see Sources, sections *a* and *d*, at pp. 148, 151).

[3] Gillies, preface p. vii.

[4] MacCulloch (1824), iii 144-5. Mrs Ramsay, Port Charlotte, kindly helped towards indentification.

[5] Donald Buchanan, *Reflections on the Isle of Barra* (London 1942), 59-60.

[6] *cf.* Muir (1861), 189.

[7] Wakehurst, xxix-xxx, 135.

changed from Norse to Gaelic within comparatively recent times[8]; while for 'Eisell ellan', or 'Laich Ile' [51], off Jura, the Norse Pladda (= flat isle) has evidently replaced the Gaelic. A more familiar change is that of Sanda [10], whose pre-Norse name is preserved in Gaelic still as Ābhainn.[8] I am told that 'Buya beg' [171], presumably representing Fuidheidh Beag, was formerly the name of the little island known as Eilean Sheumais (James's Island), after a fugitive found there by the crew of a boat that went to cut seaweed.[9] Ellan Cloich [58], with its 'pillar-shaped rock, 72 feet high, which is conspicuous from the northward and eastward', has been reasonably identified with that illustrated on the title-page of Pennant's second *Tour*, which he called 'Durisfuire'.[10] Garvhelach skean and Garvhelach na monaodh [21, 22] are the islands between Lunga and the Isles of the Sea now known as Eilean Dubh Beag and Eilean Dubh Mor.[11] An identification of 'Ellan Charne' [71] is suggested elsewhere.[12]

Balfour's 'Ronin' [126], a miscopying for 'Roum', was welcomed by Scott in preference to Rum, 'a name which a poet may be pardoned for avoiding if possible'.[13] Presumably also through a copyist's error, 'Cransay' appears for Oransay [143] in *Bal.* and *Macf.*, and in all printed editions except Hume Brown's.

Other names besides those of islands have changed since Monro's time. 'Loch Stafart' in Mull [100, line 22] is the modern Loch na Keal, or Loch-nan-ceall,[14] and 'Loch Leafan' is now Loch Scridain.

An island which no longer exists is Monro's 'Ellan

[8] Watson (1926), 91.
[9] Information from J. L. Campbell of Canna.
[10] Pennant, 417; Campbell Steven, *The Island Hills* (London 1955), 81, 86, 87.
[11] MacCulloch (1819), ii 161, map at iii 77.
[12] See Note A: Island Castles (p. 121).
[13] *Lord of the Isles*, canto iv.
[14] Mackinnon, in *Scotsman*, 11 Nov. 1887.

Slait' [33], identified by a local historian as 'probably Eilan-a-beithich' (island of birches). Only about two acres in extent, it 'has long ago disappeared, not by submergence, but by being excavated into a huge quarry, the rocky shell alone being left'.[15] This small island occupied the centre of the channel between Easdale and Seil, now almost filled with rubbish and slate refuse; its name is preserved in the village of Ellanbeich on the Seil side of the channel, where a great quarry was flooded during a storm in 1881.[16]

Monro mentions at least one place which was an island in the sense in which Kintyre was sometimes so called—that is, it was *nearly* surrounded by the sea. Carrik-steach [see Avoin, 10]—has led to some confusion; it is numbered separately as an island in all three copies of Monro's MS., and in all previous printed editions, but it is significant that Buchanan (who gives the name of every other island in Monro's list) does not mention it. Carraig Sgeith is indeed the name of a half-submerged rock some distance from the Kintyre shore[17]; but there is no such island on which a castle could be built, and no evidence in history of any such castle. Mr Andrew McKerral, C.I.E., author of *Kintyre in the Seventeenth Century*, suggests that Monro refers to Dunaverty, which had a castle with a well-authenticated history; the 'little water, wherein there is ane gude heavin for small boats', would be the Waterfoot of Dunaverty, the estuary of the Conieglen Water, which served as a local harbour from which boats set out for Irish and Lowland ports.[18]

Although not every rock or islet in the Hebrides finds a place in Monro's list, its completeness is remarkable when we consider the difficulties of travel in his day—and even in our own. Among the smallest which he mentions is Eilean a' Bhealaich [Ellan Wellich, 16], in the strait between Scarba

[15] Gillies, 10, 15.

[16] Hugh Shedden, *The Story of Lorn, its Isles and Oban* (Oban 1938), 107.

[17] *The Place Names of the Parish of Southend* (Kintyre Antiquarian Society, Campbeltown 1938).

[18] Information from Mr McKerral, and his *Kintyre*, 58-9.

and Lunga—' though a mere rock, a perfect fairyland of ferns and flowers, and warm grassy nooks '.[19] It is worth noting, however, that Monro makes no mention of the so-called Sgeir na Bain-tigherna, or Lady's Rock, lying at the southern entrance to the Sound of Mull. Every tourist is told the traditional story of the attempt by Lachlan Cattanach Maclean of Duart (who died in 1523) to dispose of his wife on this tidal rock,[20] but one historian of the clan has observed that if Monro had heard that the chief of the Macleans had tried to drown his wife on it, it is exceedingly probable that he would have stated that there was such a rock, and that he would, also, have mentioned the circumstances from which it derived its name '.[21]

Monro's *Description* does not include Rockall, 191 miles west of St Kilda, which appears first in a map of 1586, nor Argyll's ' unfound isle '.[22] In noticing St Kilda, one of Buchanan's translators (Monipennie) says ' this Hirta is the last and farther isle of Albion; so that betwixt the Isle of Man, being the first isle in Albion, and this isle, there is 377 miles'; this statement is not in Buchanan's book, and it seems to be taken from Hector Boece or Bishop Leslie.[23] The distance between Man and St Kilda is actually less than 300 English statute miles.

* * *

Of the 251 islands listed by Monro, I have been unable to identify 27, and a further 23 cannot be regarded as certain. The modern names, as well as Monro's, will be found in the index at the end of this book; for convenience I have given

[19] Muir (1861), 135; (1885), 18.

[20] *O.P.S.*, ii (i) 310 note, 313; John Mackechnie, *The Clan Maclean* (1954), 7.

[21] Sinclair, 89. The Lady's Rock was formerly called ' Leisker ' or ' Leith Sgeir ' (*H.P.*, ii 99; Marquess of Lorne, *Adventures in Legend* (1898), 146).

[22] Map of Western Europe in L. J. Waghenaer, *Speculum Nauticum* (Leyden 1586), preserved in Maps Room of British Museum (information from Dr A. B. Taylor). Introduction, p. 29. Other islands which do not appear in Monro's list are mentioned at pp. 116, 120, 125, 130.

[23] Quoted in Hume Brown, *Scotland before 1700*, 88, 154.

them as they appear in the current *West Coast Pilot* or the Ordnance Survey maps, although the spellings there (especially of Gaelic names) are not always either more consistent or more accurate than Monro's.

The following is a list of the 'hard core' of which identification has been found doubtful or impossible. The first name or names in each case is that in the Sibbald copy of Monro's MS., and where other versions may throw some further light they have also been given. The areas in which these islands may likely be found are indicated, but it is possible that this guidance may, owing to misplacing, not always be strictly correct.

Off the coast of Lorne

26. Ellan a mhadi, or Wolfis Ile.

28. Ellan vickeran. ? In Balvicar Bay, Isle of Seil.

33. Ellan Slait. Probably Eilean-a-beithich (see p. 114), near Easdale.

34. Ellan Nagvisog.

36. Iniskenzie. Inche Kenyth *BM*. Skennia *Buch*.

37. Ellan anthian. Inchian *BM*. Thiana *Buch*. Not in Pont's map of Lorn (Blaeu 115). See note G, p. 136.

38. Ellan Uderga.

41. Ellan naheglis, Kirk Ile. Eilean na Cille is shown on modern maps at the mouth of Loch Craignish. Monro does not mention Eilean More at the mouth of Loch Sween, with its church of St Charmaig or Mac-Cormaig.

42. Ellan Chriarache. Triaracha *Buch*. There is an Eilean Treadhrach off Oronsay of Colonsay (*W.C.P.* 134).

43. Ellan ard, hich Ile.

44. Ellan Iisall, laich Ile.

45. Glass Ellan, green Ile.

46. Freuch Ellan, heder Ile.

47. Ellan na cravich. Hassile or Hasil Iyle, Ellan na Crawiche *BM*. Arboraria *Buch*.

Near Lismore, Loch Linnhe

56. Iuichair, Ferray Ile. Insula Traiectus *Buch.* The name is now unknown, but the Rev. Ian Carmichael suggests the small island immediately in front of the present Lismore Ferry slipway. Blaeu (p. 115) has 'Ylen na poirt or na Nemoohir' off north end of Lismore.

57. Garbh Ellan, Roch Ile. Insula Ouicularis *Buch.* Blaeu's 'Garvellan' appears to be the modern Eilean Dubh.

60. Grezay. Gressa *Buch.* Mr Carmichael suggests Greag, S.W. of Pladda—Kreig in Blaeu, Creag in modern maps.

61. Ellan Moir, great Ile. This may be the larger of the islands opposite Kilcheran in S.E. Lismore, now called Eilean nan Gamban or Gamhna (Stirk Island).

62. Ardiasgar. 'The fisherman's height or point'.

66. Ellan drynachai. Drinacha *Buch.* Lies N.E. of Ramsay Isle, to which Monro's particulars more rightly apply (Carmichael).

Off Islay (see p. 112)

72. Ellan na caltin, Hessil Ile. Colurna *Buch.* Hume Brown asks—'Is this the Eilean Craobach of the Survey?'

77. Ellan Isall, laich Ile; Isallach *sec. manu.* Hume Brown asks—'Is this Iseanach?' (Iseanach Mor).

79. Ellan Nabeathi.

82. Ellan na naosg, Myresnyppis Ile. 'Myresnypes (which is like a Fieldfare) called Heatherbleet'—Sibbald, 'Collections of papers and informations in order to the description of Scotland' (Nat. Lib. MS. 33.5.15), p. 228.

83. Ellan Rinard, Ile of the Ness point. Ellan-rynd-nahard *BM.* Rinarda *Buch.* Also mentioned under Islay [70].

84. Liach Ellan, Lyart Ile. Cana *Buch.*

86. Auchnarra. Achnarra *Buch.*, *BM.*

93. Usabrast.

96. Ellan na bany, Webstaris Ile. Insula Textoris *Buch.*

N.B.—Pont's map of Islay (Blaeu 139) shows a string of islands off the S.W. coast of Islay; the names are so like Monro's that they may well have been taken from Buchanan's *History*. Most of them lie between McArthur's Head and the Mull of Oa, but Monro's 93-5 are near 'Ylen Ardnaw' and his 96 on the opposite side of the entrance to Loch Gruinart.

Near Iona

106. Ellan murudhain. Ellan moroan *BM*. Rudana *Buch.* 'This is probably the island on the northern extremity [of Iona], now called *Eilean Annraidh*' (Reeves, p. cxlv). Hume Brown asks—'Is this the Eilean Rabach of Ordnance Survey, or the Eilean Annraidh of Reeves's map?' Not in Blaeu.

107. Ellan Reryng. Ellan Reringe *BM*. Reringa *Buch.* Bernira *Buch.M*, 1603, 1612, and Balfour's 'Shires' MS., no. 104. Unidentified by Reeves (p. cxlv) and Mackinnon (*Scotsman*, 11 Nov. 1887). 'Possibly the modern Reidh eilean' (Hume Brown), N.W. of Iona. 'Rering' is marked in Pont's map of Mull (Blaeu 141) as a large island west of Iona, and about half its size. (A suggestion that this may be Staffa—W. C. Dendy, *The Wild Hebrides*, 1859, p. 32—is now disposed of.)

Off Skye

134. Ellan Naguyneyne. Ellan Nagoyneyne, Cunninges or Conings Ile *BM*. Cunicularia *Buch.* Identified by Hume Brown as 'Mackenzie Island', which appears neither in *W.C.P.* nor on maps. Pont's map of Skye (Blaeu 145) marks 'Ylen na Gunnur' in the modern Sound of Sleat between Kean Loch na Dallach (Skye) and Castle Ylen

Donnen. Monro's phrase 'foiranent Loch Ailis' suggests Glas Eilean between Ardintoul and Avernish (Lochalsh).

142/3. The note supplied from *BM* may refer to Fladda-chuain (238); Sibbald's own 'Description' says (p. 33):— 'Troda is ane isle at the north point of Sky'.

145-9. Unnamed islands, probably in Loch Bracadale. *Buch.* gives 'Buia parua deinde Buia maior', and Ordnance Survey shows also Harlosh Island and Tarner Island. Pont's map has Oransa, Vya beg, Via moir at mouth of Loch Brakadil.

150-2. Pont's map names seven islands in Loch Faillord (the old name for Loch Dunvegan) inside 'Ylen Isa', as follows:—Yl. Cholbesk, Yl. Gravellan, Ylen Clash, Yl. Grinen, Yl. Heuf, Yl. Garra, Yl. Skiandel. O.S. map names Gairbh Eilean, Eilean Mor and Eilean Dubh.

Off Barra

162. Scarpnamult. Scarpa Vervecum *Buch.* Rev. Edward Macqueen, in *O.S.A.* xiii (1794), 328 note, identified this with Lianamul, off Mingulay, but Mr J. L. Campbell agrees that it is Maol Domhnaich, 'a very suitable island for grazing wethers'.

171. Buya beg. Probably Fuidheidh Beag, now named Eilean Sheumais, James's Island, after a fugitive from the mainland (J. L. Campbell); Hume Brown says 'Udhay'.

172. Buya moir. Probably Fuiay (pronounced 'Wia', *W.C.P.* 321).

173. Hay.

Sound of Harris

186. Soa. Hume Brown identifies with Shillay.

199. Heyia. Perhaps Tahay?

200. Hoya. There is a peninsula called Hoe Beg.

201. Ferelay.

205-6. Seuna beg, Seuna moir. Shown at S.E. corner of Harris in Blaeu, p. 149.

N.B.—The following larger islands in the Sound of Harris have not been identified in Monro's list:—Shillay, Boreray, Lingay, Torogay, Stromay (N. Uist), Vatersay, Sursay, Vaccasay.

Off Harris and Lewis

208-9. Slegain, Tuemen. Blaeu (p. 149) shows ' Slegan beg ' and ' Slegan M.' and ' Tueme ' between ' Taransa ' and ' Skarpa '.

212-13. Garvellan, Lambay. Blaeu shows them south of Flada, at the mouth of Loch Roag.

227. Ellan Adam. Perhaps Eilean na Crotach, off Eye Peninsula.

233. Ere, Irland. Erin *Blaeu*.

240. Senchastell, auld castell. Apparently Eilean Mhuire, Shiant Isles. Blaeu (p. 149) includes Yl. Sheni, Shen Chast. beg, Shen Chastel Moir, and Fladda in the Shiant group. Muir (1861) in his map opp. p. 168, gives ' Seann Chaisteal ' as the name of a rock off the east end of Eilean Mhuire.

Loch Broom

244. Ellan af vill. Afulla *Buch.* Not in Blaeu (p. 117). Perhaps Eilean Dubh, between Priest Island and Tanera More, or the group which includes it, where the islands are separated by Na Feadh 'laichean (plural of *feadhail*, a variant of *faodhail*, an extensive beach—Watson, 1904, p. 260).

Note A. ISLAND CASTLES

Monro is so particular in listing the castles in the Isles which existed in his day that it is worth seeing what fresh light is shed on their location by the *Description* as now printed.

From it I think we can identify the rendezvous fixed by Donald Dubh, claimant to the Lordship of the Isles, for those who supported him in the rebellion of 1545. It was at 'Ellancarne' (according to documents which are still preserved) that the 'Barons and Council of the Isles' met on 28 July of that year, and appointed commissioners to treat with Henry VIII, before sailing to Knockfergus in Ireland, where they were with 4000 men and 180 galleys on 5 August (Gregory, 170).

Ellan Charne [71], at the mouth of the Sound of Islay, has probably escaped the notice of historians by being listed in previous editions of Monro's *Description* as 'Earne Isle', as it appears in the Balfour and Macfarlane MSS. But the meaning of the name is plain from Buchanan: '*inter Ilam, & Iuram sita est insula parua a cumulo lapidum cognominata*'. It appears to be the island now known as Am Fraoch Eilean, off the south end of Jura, where Pennant was told that the Macdonalds once had a castle. The Welsh traveller's account of it in 1772 cannot be bettered:—

> 'After dinner [with Archibald Campbell of Jura] walk down to the sound of *Ilay*, and visit the little island of *Fruchlan*, near to the shore, and a mile or two from the eastern entrance. On the top is a ruined tower of a square form, with walls nine feet thick ; on the West side the rock on which it stands is cut through to a vast depth, forming a foss over which had been the drawbridge. This fortress seemed as if intended to guard the mouth of the sound ; and was also the prison where the *Mac-donalds* kept their captives, and in old times was called the castle of *Claig*.' (Pennant, i 246.)

This was apparently the island prison to which the Earl and Countess of Athol were taken by Angus, son of the last Lord of the Isles, in the reign of James III (Anderson, 356; Islay (1850), 15; Gregory, 54; Tytler, ii 192). There are anchorages for large vessels near the island (*W.C.P.*, 140-1) and at Whitefarland Bay at the other entrance to the Sound, where the French Admiral Thurot lay during his descents on these coasts in 1759-60 Pennant, i 269; *P.S.A.S.*, v 364-8).

I can find no good reason for the suggestion that 'Ellan-carne' of the records was the same as or near the Isle of Eigg (*State Papers*, i 53; *Clan Donald*, i 372, 399), beyond the fact that the Council of the Isles may have met there once before, and that Sir James Macdonald was received with ceremonious rejoicing in Eigg on his way to Islay in 1615 (R. Pitcairn, *Ancient Criminal Trials in Scotland*, iii/1 20). The only 'defensive construction' on Eigg listed by the Royal Commission on Ancient Monuments is a nameless fort on the Scuir (9th Report, 220-1).

* * *

Regarding the four great castles on record as belonging to the Lord of the Isles in the 14th century, the evidence of Monro's *Description* is less satisfactory.

In 1343, David II granted to John of Yle the keeping of the royal castles ('*custodias castrorum nostrorum*') of Kerno-borgh, Iselborgh and Dunchonall, with the lands and small isles belonging to them (*A.P.S.*, xii 6; Robertson, 99, 100). In 1354, John of Lorn, Lord of Argyle, relinquished to John of Yle, Lord of the Isles, his claim to the castles of Kerneburch and Hystylburch, with all their islands and rights, and the castle of Dunconill, with all its pertinents, stipulating that the keeping of the castle of Kerneburch should never be given to any of the clan Fynwyne, or Mackinnon (*H.P.*, i 75-8). In 1390, Donald de Ile, Lord of the Isles, granted to Lachlan Maclean of

Duart two charters, the one conveying half of the constabulary of the castles of Dunconail and Dunkerd, with the isle of Gerbealach, the two islands of Garbealan and Scealda, &c.; and the other conveying the constabulary and keeping of his castles of Kernaborg and Isleborg, together with the small isles of Floda and Lunga (*R.M.S.*, ii 480). Writing about 1380, John of Fordun mentions two of these castles—'the great castle of Dunquhonle' near Garveleane, and 'Carneborg, an exceeding strong castle' four miles by sea from Mull (quoted Brown, 14).

These last two castles are easily identified with Monro's 'Kerniborg' [114]—which appears for the first time in the present edition—and 'Dunchonill' [25]. Both islands are ringed with high cliffs: on the one are considerable remains of fortifications (Beveridge, *Coll and Tiree*, 61-6), but the other is grass-grown to the summit, and now 'sheep pasture where kings trod' (Seton Gordon, *Highways and Byways of the West Highlands*, 320; Campbell Steven, *The Island Hills*, 100).

Regarding Iselborgh, Hystylburch or Isleborg (not mentioned by Fordun), *O.P.S.* (ii 322 note) says it 'seems to be unknown', while Beveridge says there is 'certainly every probability' that it was in either the Treshnish Isles or Tiree (p. 119 note). The first element in the name is probably Old Irish *isel*, Gaelic *iosal*, 'low', and Dr A. B. Taylor suggests that it may be the older name for Cairn na Burgh Beg, where the fortifications are at a lower level than on Cairn na Burgh More. In Tiree, the two sites favoured by Beveridge are Dun Ibrig, near Baugh, which was surrounded by a marsh said still to become a loch in winter, or the ancient castle which stood in Loch an Eilean at Heylipol (pp. 112, 118); the Skye seneachie's history of the Macdonalds (*H.P.*, i 59), says that Sir Donald *Galdach* of Lochalsh 'went to Tyree, and died in the Inch of Teinlipeil', a name which—although now unknown there—may have been a form of Heylipol, as Beveridge suggests.

As to Dunkerd, mentioned in the 1390 charter only, there is no clue in Monro. The locations given by Gregory (p. 69)—' Dunconnell, in Scarba, and Dunkerd, in the Garveloch Isles '—are not in accordance with *R.M.S.* quoted above, and both castles seem to have been in the same area.

* * *

A puzzling question about the number of castles in Skye in Monro's day arises from the inclusion of Dunringill, overlooking Loch Slapin, in his list [132]. Although it is one of six which he names, he gives the total number as only five, thus contradicting himself but agreeing with Buchanan (although Aikman's translation raises it to seven) and with a document compiled apparently about 1613. An official list of ' Houses in the Isles ' (*Register of the Privy Council of Scotland*, ed. David Masson 1891, x 821) contains this statement: ' Of stane houses in the Sky thair is fyve, to wit:—Duntilloun in Trouternes, being ane pairt of the Sky possessd by Donald Gorme without richt; Dunvaigen in the Sky, perteaning to Macloyde of Hairish; Donnakine, perteaning to Makenon in the Sky; Dunruissil, perteaning also to Makinon; Caymes in Slait, perteaning to Donald Gorme; Duniskaith in Slait, perteaning to Donald Gorme '. Here is the same discrepancy which we find in Monro, except that ' Dunruissil ' has replaced ' Dunringill ' (which, to make things more confusing, is shown as an alternative name for Duntulm in Blaeu's map). Did the writer of 1613 know Monro's account, and was a sixth name added, or mentioned in some way that showed it was not one of the five castles? Its inclusion has led a recent writer to assume that in those days some of the strongholds in the islands may have been little more than duns or brochs such as Dunringill (James Macintyre, *Castles in Skye*, 13), but the discrepancy noted above suggests that it would be rash to draw such a definite conclusion.

Regarding Pabay [222], the refuge of MacLeod of Lewis at the mouth of Loch Roag, a legal document at Dunvegan dated 1527 says:—'Alexander MacLeod dwelleth in the isles where the Officers of the law dare not pass for hazard of their lives' (MacLeod, 28); and in the following century, it was stated, 'the ordnar place of Macloyds residence, in this countrey was Pappa ane Island within the sea' (Macfarlane, ii 532). Near Pabay More is Bearasay (not mentioned by Monro), a precipitous island off the west end of Great Bernera, with the foundations of a few houses close together; there Neil MacLeod of Lewis held out for three years before his execution in 1613, and it was described as 'a fort invincible, unto the which Neill wes accustomed some yeirs to send alwayes provision of victualls, and other things necessarie, that it might be a retreat unto him upon all occasions in tyme of his greatest necessitie' (Sir R. Gordon, *A Genealogical History of the Earldom of Sutherland*, Edin. 1813, 275; Ancient Monts., 9th report, 30).

Note B. RELIGIOUS HOUSES

In spite of the criticisms of Dr MacCulloch, there are some interesting references in Monro's *Description* to church buildings and religious houses in his day. It should be borne in mind that he was writing about the time of the Reformation, and that his account did not see the light of day until after that event. From the use of the past tense in references to the Bishops of Argyll and of the Isles, it almost seems that it was revised after 1560.

There are records to support Monro's mention of the Isle of Man [1] as that 'whereinto is the Cathedral Kirk of the Bishoproy of Man and Isles dedicat in the honour of Peter Apostle' (this was at Peel), while the Abbey of Iona [103] 'was the Cathedral Kirk that the Bischoppis of the Iles had sen the time thai were banist out of the Ile of man be the Inglismen'. In Lismore [53] was 'ane paroche kirk quhilk sumtime was the cathedrall kirk set of the Bischop of Argyle', and on a nearby isle [66], Monro tells us, were 'auld mansis, quhair habitation of Bischops & Nobles were in auld times'. The contemporary Thomas-Skene MS. (Skene iii 435-6) speaks of Monro's 'Achaadn or Bell buacheir' on Lismore as 'the castell of Auchindewne, upon the west side thairof anent the Mule, quhilk wes biggit be ane Bischope of the Iles' [*sic*]; there was a castle or manor there in 1304, and the ruin still to be seen has been identified as that of the palace of the ancient Bishops (*O.P.S.*, ii 169; Anderson, 312; Rev. Ian Carmichael, *Lismore in Alba*, 122-3).

Returning to Iona, Monro mentions 'ane Abbay [*Bal.*, *Macf.* have 'monastery'] of Monks and ane Monasterie of Nunnis'—*cf.* Gordon, p. iii, where he criticises Queen Victoria for saying 'there had been two monasteries there', on the grounds that one was a nunnery. As the property of the Abbot, Monro speaks of an island in 'Loch Sterotsa' in Islay [70], Soay, Eilean nam Ban, 'Ellan Murudhain' and 'Ellan Reryng' [104-7], and Canna [129]; while belonging to the Prioress of Iona were the isle and parish of Inchkenneth [108], Eorsa [109], and Heisker or Monach [182]. The Thomas-Skene MS. (Skene iii 431) says 'Helsker . . . payis yeirlie to the monasterie of Colmkill, to whom it apperteins, 60 bollis victuall by other customis'. Monro also records that in Oronsay [97] was 'ane Monasterie of Channonis'; at Rodil in Harris [249] 'ane Monasterie with ane steipill, quhilk was foundit and biggit be M^cloyd of Haray'; and on Holy Island, or Molass, off Arran [5], 'there was foundit be John of the Isles ane Monasterie of Friars which is decayed'.

The 'Monasterie' in Oronsay of Colonsay (Thomas-Skene MS. calls it 'an Abbay place') was actually a priory, and when Monro was Archdeacon of the Isles the prior was Donald Macduffie (died 1554), whose effigy remains to illustrate the costume of the period (Pennant, plate xx, opp. i 271; Wakehurst, plate xxvi, between 70-1; George Scott Moncrieff, *The Scottish Islands*, 1952, p. 26, fig. 16).

The tomb, and the little chapel on the south of the church still known as the Prior's chapel, may have been erected by the 'gentle captain' named by Monro (Murray, 169-70). The prior is vested; his head rests on a pillow beneath a Gothic canopy; his right hand is raised in the act of benediction; his left grasps his pastoral staff; around it is the inscription '*hic jacet Dns Donaldus Macdu*[*ffie*] [*prior de Or*]*an*[*s*]*ay* [*obiit an*]*no MDL.*'

Monro's reference to Rodil has been much discussed. The Rev. John Macleod, minister of Harris, wrote about 1794:—'Buchanan says, the monastery of Rowdill was built by Alexander Macleod of Harris, but this is an egregious mistake. The church of the monastery was only repaired by this Alexander Macleod, who died, as the inscription on his tomb bears, A.D. 1527. There is not a stone left in the foundation of the priory. The place of it cannot now be traced, and all we surely know of it is, that it once has been' (*Stat. Acc.*, x 378-9; see also Muir (1885), 273). The Royal Commission on Ancient Monuments reported that Monro's 'is the earliest reference to the place, and the Dean would seem to be using monastery like "minster" as equivalent to a church. There is no other evidence of a monastic establishment or of any ancient use of the term "priory"; while in 1561 among the parsonages pertaining to the Bishop of the Isles is reckoned "the personage of Roidill in Harris"' (Ninth Report, 37). Canon MacLeod, however, inclined to the opinion 'that the Dean meant what he said, and that, though there is no evidence that there was a monastery at Rodil in Culdee days, there really was one there in the Middle Ages' (p. 49).

The monastery on Holy Island has also been said to have been founded by Reginald MacSomerled towards the end of the 12th century, and it may have been re-established by the 'Good John of Isla' (M'Arthur, 180-1; V. A. Firsoff in *The Scotsman*, 8 March 1952; but see also Murray, 153-4). It seems to have been on the north-west side of the island, but recent excavations have revealed no trace of it except for some glazed pebbles, often associated with medieval buildings.

Monro mentions Bernera [64] off Lismore and the Flannan Isles [211] as 'holy girths', but Bishop Dowden pointed out (*Church*, 150) that all claims for the privilege of sanctuary put forward on behalf of places in the Western Highlands and Islands should be accepted with hesitation.

Note C. THE BISHOP'S ISLES

Monro mentions thirteen islands, and one islet, as pertaining to the Bishop of the Isles in property. They were Eilean nan Each [127], Muck [128], Raasay [138], Rona [139], nine of the isles south of Barra [156-64], and an islet in Loch Moyburg in Islay [170]. His list can be added to by reference to the Thomas-Skene MS. of the same period.

Martin, in his *Description* written about 1695 and first published in 1703, speaks in particular of the Barra Isles as being 'commonly called the Bishop's Isles, because they are held by the Bishop' (1934 edn., 162). They are so described in some of the early maps, and as late as the 1880's Dr Alexander Carmichael found that 'the head of this wild precipitous chain of islands is still called Bearnaraidh an Easpig, Bearnarey of the Bishop, occasionally Barra Head' (*Crofters Commission*, 456).

As stated in Monro's own account of Raasay and Rona, the Bishop did not always have peaceful possession of his property. In *Acta Dominorum Concilii et Sessionis*, under date 14 March 1532/3, this record occurs:—'Compeirit ane Reuerend fader in God, Ferquhar, Bischop of the Ilis and Commendatour of Colmekyll, and constitut Procuratour Maister Jhone Lethame, *cum totis Procuratoribus curie*, in the actioun movit be him aganis M'Neile the Lard of Barray, MacGillechallum callit of Rasay, and in all uther actionis,' &c. (quoted Iona Club, 3-4; Maclean, 67; Gordon, 96).

In addition to the Bishop's Isles listed by Monro, the following references in the Thomas-Skene MS. may be noted:—*Oronsay* [97]—' It is 4 merk land, quhairin is but ane town, quhilk is an Abbay place dedicat to St Columb: it partenis to the Bischop of the Iles ' (Skene, iii 438); *Mull* [100]—' The Bischop hes 30 merk land thair, but Maclane Doward hes it in his possessioun occupeit be his kin ' (Skene, iii 434); *Muck* [128]—' It pertenis also to the foirsaid Bischop, and is possest be the Laird of Ardinmwrthe callit Maken. It is four merk land, and payis to the said Laird and his Factors aucht score bollis victuall, quhairof fourscore to the Bischop and fourscore to the Laird ' (Skene, iii 434); *Canna* [129]—' It pertenis to the Bischop of the Iles, but the said Clan-Rannald hes it in possessioun ' (Skene, iii 434). Monro says of Canna that ' It perteins to the Abbot of Colmkill'; which agrees with the 1561 rental.

Note D. ISLAND SPORTS

The old method of hunting deer, referred to by Monro as being practised in Jura [14] and Rum [126], is discussed by the late Professor W. J. Watson in *The Celtic Review* for 1913-14. He there explains that ' the term " tinchell " . . . means the body of men, sometimes numbering thousands, who drove the deer into the elrig or eilearg, and seems to be rather a loose use of *timchioll*, a circuit '.

The Rev. Donald M'Lean, minister of the Small Isles, wrote about 1796:—' Before the use of fire arms, their method of killing deer was as follows: On each side of a glen, formed by two mountains, stone dykes were begun pretty high in the mountains, and carried to the lower part of the valley, always drawing nearer, till within 3 or 4 feet of each other. From this narrow pass, a circular space was inclosed by a stone wall, of a height sufficient to confine the deer; to this place they were pursued and destroyed. The vestige of one of these inclosures is still to be seen in Rum' (*Stat. Acc.*, xvii 275). This method of hunting will recall the 'Khedda' to those familiar with sport in India.

Regarding Monro's account of killing seals at Traigh Gruinard, in Islay [70], this sport has long been forgotten there, and the use of dogs does not seem to be known elsewhere (Anderson, 363; 'Gowrie', 277; Seton Gordon, *Highways and Byways of the West Highlands*, 312). There are many references to seal-killing on Haskeir [183]—not to be confused with the Monach group of the same name ten miles to the south—and on Causamul (thus in *W.C.P.*, 342, also found as Colsmon, Collismown, Causmoun, Collinar skyr, Cosmel—not in Monro), off the west coast of North Uist—see Thomas-Skene MS., in Skene, iii 431; Dymes, in Mackenzie, 594; Martin, 133; Scott, canto i; *New Stat. Acc.*, xiv 164; Beveridge, 295 note.

Monro's numerous references to fishing may be compared with the Thomas-Skene MS., which describes the people of Harris 'as unskilfull in slaying of the fishes and salmond that cummis as thair neighbours are' (Skene, iii 430); the St Kildians 'make na labour to obtene or slay ony fisches, but gadderis sum in the craigis, albeit thai micht have abundance thairof utherwayis gif thai wald only way make labour thairfore' (Skene, iii 431-2); but in Skye 'thair is great plentie of salmond and hering tane' (Skene, iii 433). The method of catching sea fish by the erection of stone dykes across tidal waters, described by Monro in his account of Loch Bee in South Uist [180], 'was used until its suppression by 19th century factors engaged in the zealous protection of salmon and sea trout' (information from Mr J. L. Campbell of Canna). Mention by Buchanan of the dyke being 60 feet broad is not in any of the Monro MSS., but Sibbald's own 'Description' (p. 38) speaks of 'a thick dyke of some threescore of foot made to keep it [the sea] out'; *Buch.* 1690 has 'a Jitty or Bank of Sixty Foot high' (*sic*).

Falconry or hawking was still a popular pastime in Monro's day, although it was complained in 1551 that noblemen could not exercise it as in times past (*A.P.S.*, ii 483, and index vol. xii, *s.v.* Hawk). Monro tells of falcons' or hawks' nests in Islay [70], Coll [120], Muck [128], Canna [129], Lingay [156], Greanamul ['Gigarmen', 157], 'Scarpay na Mult' [162], Orosay [166], Flodday [170], 'Buya moir' [172, ? Fuday], Uist [180], St Kilda [184], and Lewis and Harris [249]. James IV, in a charter to MacLeod dated 1498, reserved the eyries and falcons' nests (MacLeod, 60), and he sent his falconer to Lewis for hawks in 1508 and to the Isles in 1512 (*Accounts*, iv 118, 346).

According to Monro, solan geese (or gannets) were found on Ailsa Craig [2], Rum [126], and Eigg [130], but on St Kilda [184] and Sula Sgeir [251] he only speaks of 'wild fowl'. The custom which he mentions of men from Ness in Lewis going annually to Sula Sgeir for young birds still continues after 400 years (Stewart, 39-47; Atkinson, 281-313; *The Scotsman*, 14 Aug. 1954, and letters by Seton Gordon, R. M. Lockley, &c., in issues of 24 Nov. 1938, 2 Jan. 1939, &c.); its object is more practical than mere sport, as is shown by the framing of a special order under the Protection of Birds Act, 1954, to allow gannets to be killed or taken on Sula Sgeir outside the close season (*The Scotsman*, 18 Feb. 1955). Regarding Rum and Eigg, where no gannets breed today, Monro may have referred to Manx shearwaters, for both birds are sometimes used for human food (inf. from Messrs Seton Gordon and J. L. Campbell; J. D. L. in *The Scotsman*, 20 Aug. 1949).

Note E. BARRA 'COCKLES'

It is significant to find—for the first time—the Barra [165] 'cockle' story attributed to Hector Boece, the father of many of the legends in Scottish history. His name is not mentioned in the Balfour and Macfarlane MSS., and Monro and Buchanan have suffered ridicule for giving it apparently on their own authority.

It is of Mull, and not of Barra, that Boece tells the story in his *History* (1527):—'In this Ile of Mule is ane cleir fontane, two millis fra the see: fra this fontane discendis ane litil burne, or strip, rinnand ful of rounis [roe of fish] to the seis. Thir rounis ar round and quhit, schinand like perle, full of thik humour; and, within two houris eftir that thay come to see, they grow in gret cocles' (Bellenden's translation, quoted Brown, 87-8). Bishop Leslie, in whose *Historie of Scotland* (first published in 1578) there are several acknowledgments to Boece in the description of the Hebrides, says of Mull:—'We undirstand, as we haue hard say, that in it is a fontane twa myles distante frome the Sey, out of quhilke egis verie small, schineng as cleir as a pretious margarite, flowis intil a certane bosum of salt water on the sey syd, quhair in the space of xii. [*sic*] houris thay grow in fair cokilis or bukies' (Leslie, i 57).

Like Monro, the author of the Thomas-Skene MS. attaches the story to Barra:—'Item in this Ile is ane weill quhairin growis cockles, quhilk is at the fute [*sic*] of ane hill callit the hill of Barra, twa mile fra the sea' (Skene, iii 430). Another anonymous account of Barra, dated between 1613-22, says:—'There is one litle springand fresh water running out of ane grein hill above the Church, which doeth flow into the sea, and there is springand there certane litill Cockles shells which they alladge that the samen doth flow into the sea out of the Well and doeth grow in another place next the Church not the tenth part of ane myll from the church of Barray called Killbarray' (*Spot. Misc.*, ii 353; Macfarlane, ii 529; Campbell, 43, 44). Martin says in his account of Barra:—'they say that the Well of Kilbarr throws up embryoes of cockles, but I could not discern any in the rivulet, the air being at that time foggy' (p. 158).

So persistent has been this story, or superstition, that two Presbyterian ministers of Barra have taken the trouble to ridicule it. The Rev. Edward Macqueen wrote about 1794:—'Buchanan is undoubtedly mistaken, when he asserts, that the cockle originated from small animalculi coming down along with the water of a spring at the top of a green hill above the sand. It is true, there is such a hill, with a spring on the summit of it; but any water running from it does not come to the sea, being absorbed by the intervening ground, which is sandy; besides that, it is allowed by all naturalists, that every animal procreates its own species. But this vulgar notion prevails among the inhabitants to this day' (*Stat. Acc.*, xiii 337 note). The Rev. Alex. Nicolson wrote about 1840:—'Nothing can show the credulity of the Dean more than this account of the cockles being formed in embryo on the top of a hill, in a fresh water spring, and thereafter carried down to the sea when they grow large. There certainly is such a spring yet to be seen, but no visible appearance of any thing like cockles forming there' (*New Stat. Acc.*, xiv 204-5).

In our day, one writer says the spring locally identified with the legend lies within 3 or 4 yards of the summit of Ben Eoligarry, above Traigh Mhòr, and adds:—'The water of it is charged with calcium carbonate, which is deposited on sand grains and similar objects, thus giving rise to the superstition that the water contained minute cockles' (A. A. MacGregor, *Summer Days among the Western Isles*, 276).

Note F. *THE PIGMIES' ISLE*

Monro's story that the bones of pigmies had been found in a little island off Lewis has for long been the subject of speculation. The island, which now appears on the maps as Luchruban, near the Butt of Lewis, was rediscovered and examined some 50 years ago, and Monro's character as a reliable writer vindicated, by the late Mr William Cook Mackenzie, the historian. He discussed the matter fully, and described the island and its 'pigmies kirk' in detail, in

P.S.A.S., vol. xxxix (1905), pp. 248-58 (see also his *Outer Hebrides*, 499, and *Highlands and Isles*, 159 note). 'Expert examination at South Kensington Museum,' he wrote, 'proved that the bones which local tradition attributed to a pigmy race were the bones of mammals and birds: the food, in fact, of the anchorite who had inhabited the cell.'

All the relevant information will be found in Mr Mackenzie's writings, for which the chief references are:—Skene, iii 429; Dymes, 592; Morisone, in *Spot. Misc.*, ii 342, and Macfarlane, ii 215; William Collins, 'An Ode on the Superstitions of the Highlands of Scotland' (written probably *c.* 1749, and first published in 1788); MacCulloch (1824), iii 272-4; and Miller, 350-1 and 21. Sir Robert Sibbald's own 'Description' (MS., p. 44) says that the bones 'when examined are found to be the bones of some small Fowls, which abound in that place'—a phrase almost identical with that used by John Morisone, 'indweller' in Lewis about 1680.

Modern guide-books state that the threat of the 'little men of the Luchruban' is still held out to naughty children by parents in the Ness district of Lewis.

Note G. PLACE-NAMES

Monro does not often discuss the derivation of the names of islands, although he frequently gives both the Scots and Gaelic forms; and this is sometimes a useful clue to identity as well as meaning. Some of the names are worth examining more closely.

The present text gives Skye [132] a definitely adjectival form—'Ellan Skianach'—in place of *Bal.* and *Macf.* 'Ellan Skyain' and *Buch.* 'Skiana'. Monro's translation of it as 'the wyngit Ile' is followed by Martin (p. 190), and also provisionally accepted by the modern scholars MacBain (p. 33) and Watson (1926, p. 39); although Mackinnon was not satisfied (*Scotsman*, 9 Nov. 1887). Monro no doubt had in mind the Gaelic *sgiath*, 'a wing'; but the name is perhaps older than Gaelic, as it is found in Ptolemy, *c.* A.D. 150, in the form *Skitis*. Watson suggests that *Skitis* is derived from an early Celtic word which is a root of *sgiath* and which is cognate with Latin *scindo*, *scidi*, ' I cut '. ' The cloudy island '—hence the poetic ' misty isle '—was suggested by Dr John Macpherson, minister of Sleat (p. 282 note), and from him by Pennant (i 352).

The presence of ' v ' or ' bh ' in the names of Kerrera [69], Colonsay [99, 111] and Oronsay [166] is worth noting. Of the first, Watson noted that ' in Gaelic pronunciation there is still distinct trace of *bh*—*Cear*(*bh*)*ara* ' (intro. to MacBain, p. xix); Monro's ' Colvansay ' is near the Gaelic ' *Colbhasa* ' and the original Norse ' *Kolbeins-ey* '; and on ' Orbandsay ' (' Oruansay ' *Bal.* ' Orvansay ' *Macf.*) J. L. Campbell comments: ' it is an interesting survival, corresponding to a Gaelic spelling Orbhansaidh; the present pronunciation is Oro'osaidh with distinct hiatus, not recognised by the Ordnance Survey '.

Monro's spelling ' Raarsay ' for Raasay [138] was at first thought by MacBain (pp. 102, 36) to be ' an oddity of his own '; but that it was more is suggested by the fact that the name ' is sometimes heard pronounced Raarsa ', and ' seems to stand for *Rár-áss-ey*, Isle of Roe-ridge '.

Of place-names other than those of islands, one of the most interesting is ' Loch Portrigh ' in Skye [132]. The name is said to have originated with James V's visit in 1540, only nine years before the date of Monro's own tour; but Professor Watson has suggested another derivation, from ' *righ* ' or ' *ruigh* ', ' fore-arm ', common in place-names as ' slope ', ' ground sloping up to a hill ' (1926, p. 158 note).

An example of how Monro's reputation has suffered from miscopying is found in *Sib.* ' Helsker na caillach ' [182] for *Bal.* and *Macf.* ' Helsker Nagaillon '. The former both agrees with *Buch.* ' *Helscer Vetularum* ' and supports the identification with Heisgeir nan Cailleach, and at the same time disposes of a tentative association with Clan

Maclean (Beveridge, 73). See also Carmichael, *Crofters Commission*, app. pp. 464-5, and *Carmina*, ii 375 note.

It is appropriate here to refer to the derivation given by Buchanan (although not, strangely enough, in any of the Monro MSS.) for 'Ellan anthian' [37]. This island—*Bal.* and *Macf.* Inchian, *Buch.* Thiana—seems to lie somewhere off the coast of Lorne, but it has not been identified. *Buch.* 1690 renders the original Latin as 'the isle called *Tyan*, from an Herb, which is prejudicial to Fruits, not unlike *Guild* or *Loose-strife*, but that 'tis of a more dilute Colour'; and the English edition of 1762 adds a footnote:—'the herb guild, of a deep yellow colour, frequent among corns'. *An dithean* is frequently used in a general sense for 'flower', but particularly for the corn marigold, *Chrysanthemum segetum*, known in Scotland as gules, gools, guills, or yellow gowans (John Cameron, *Gaelic Names of Plants*, 1883, 42-3; Rev. John Lightfoot, *Flora Scotica*, 2nd edn. 1792, i 489-90; J. D. Hooker, *The Student's Flora*, 1870, 202; '*gul*' is modern Danish for yellow). Lightfoot says:—'These golden flowers turn towards the sun all day, an ornament to the corn-fields, and afford a pleasing sight to the passenger, but are so very detrimental to the husbandman, that a law is in force in *Denmark*, which oblidges the inhabitants every where to eradicate them out of their grounds'.

In the present text we find rescued from oblivion the old name of the North Ford of Uist [180]—now bridged like the South Ford. The 'Faghill of Caraness' is derived from Gaelic *Faodhail*, which is itself derived from Old Norse *vaðill*, 'a ford', and the names *An Faodhail Tuath*, and the Faodhail Carinish, are still known in Benbecula.

Note H. ERRORS IN EARLIER EDITIONS

Monro's reputation for accuracy has suffered through the loss of his original MS., and before examining some of the mistakes in previous editions it is natural to ask the question: from what MS. or MSS. were they derived? Excepting the publication of Macfarlane's version in 1908, I find it impossible to say with certainty.

Apart from differences in spelling, which are not always a sure guide, I have noted six variations between the Balfour and Macfarlane MSS. which the curious may wish to examine. Comparing the hitherto accepted text with the versions given in my footnotes, the absence from the former of the words 'foulls' [126] and 'naturall' [250]—both of them in Balfour—might lead one to suppose that Macfarlane was followed; and the use of his 'Grynord' and 'Britane' [70, 126], instead of Balfour's 'Ruidarde' and 'Beltane', might seem to put the matter beyond doubt. But the presence of Balfour's 'manurit' and 'corn' [185, 207]—both omitted by Macfarlane—suggest otherwise. These points argue both against either MS. being the sole source, and against there having been any collation of the two. It may also be noted that the MS. previously founded upon contained two striking phrases appearing in Balfour and Macfarlane, but not in Sibbald—'rockie scabrous isle' [48], and 'rockie knobe' [22]. Can there have been yet another version—perhaps containing the word 'coelts' [14, see glossary p. 159]—of Monro's MS.?

Having thrown out this hint, let us examine the old text, keeping in mind the fact that none of Monro's editors appreciated the value of the Latin summary by Buchanan as a check on the original.

As was only to be expected, proper names became mutilated at the hands of copyists ignorant of Gaelic. But that carelessness (as well as ignorance) played its part is shown, for example, by finding 'Hettesay' for 'Hellesay' [174]—except in the 1908 edition—for the 'll' is certain in *Macf.*, although not quite so clear in *Bal.*, and Buchanan has 'Hellesaia'.

There are at least three instances of major errors due to careless copying which remained undetected through all the previous seven printed versions of the text. In the notice of Rum [126], Sibbald and Balfour are agreed that men gathered wild fowls' eggs ' about *Beltane* ', which has until now been misread (as indeed it appears in *Macf.*) as ' about ' *Britane* '—an error which would have been made plain by comparison with Buchanan (' quorum quantum libet quiuis *vere* adulto colliget ') or his translators. Under Rona [139], previous editions have '. . . the same havein is *guyed* [for ' quyet ' *Bal.*, *Macf.*] for fostering of theives, ruggairs, and reivairs *till a nail* ' (for ' *till await* '), which contains two misreadings of the MSS.; Hume Brown even added the ingenious footnote—' The meaning is that they carried off everything *even to a nail* '.

There is a misreading in the account of St Kilda [Hirta, 184] in all editions except 1908, which have '. . . and findis it sweeit, and *eets the* greyns after the sweeitness thereof ', although it is clearly ' and findis it sweeit, and greyines after the sweeitnes thereof ' (*Bal.*) and ' findis it seit, and greyns after the sweitness of it ' (*Macf.*); the word is therefore ' groans ' and not ' grains ' as suggested by Hume Brown.

I find only three cases where a misreading in the 1774 edition has subsequently been corrected, apart from the new text of 1908. In transcribing the account of Islay [70], the reference to Dunivaig as ' *biggit* on ane craig ' became instead ' the biggest ', but this error was corrected in the 1805 and all later editions. Two errors of 1774 had to wait until the 1893 edition by Hume Brown for correction: under Jura [14] ' in norne leid ' (= in Norse speech)—clear in all MSS.—was run together as ' innorne Leid '; and under Harris [249] ' macttickes ' appeared for ' martrickes ' of *Bal.* (and 1893 edition), or ' marticks ' of *Macf.* (' matricks ' in 1908 edition).

The 1805 edition is responsible for a few minor blunders. Probably by a printer's error, which remained unnoticed, the ' Tigsay ' [80] of 1774 became ' Tisgay ', and so it remained except in 1908 [it is actually ' Tegsay ' in *Bal.*, *Macf.*). The word ' zeirlie ' [216, line 5]—' zeirly ' in *Bal.*, ' yerly ' in *Macf.*—is omitted in all but 1774 and 1908; and the same applies to the ' of ' in ' aboundance of deir ' which *Bal.* and *Macf.* substitute for ' mony deir ' of *Sib.* under Harris [249, lines 15/16]. The 1818 edition is responsible for a further omission: the words ' ane castell in ' disappear from the notice of Barra [165, lines 9/10] both in that edition and those of 1884, 1893 and 1934.

The old style of printing ' s ' like ' f ' caused some confusion in the names of Nos. 74, 94 and 95, and there are mistakes in copying the titles of Nos. 83 and 98. Careless errors in numbering Nos. 50 and 211 [old Nos. 51 and 193]—the same mistake in 1818 and 1884—will be observed; and it is curious to find the serial number and title of Man [1], which appear in all three MSS., and in the first edition, dropped from 1805 onwards, and only restored in 1908 and 1934.

To sum up, therefore, it appears that later editors not only failed to seek out the MS. sources, but did not even trouble to check their texts with the earliest edition. The 1818 editor took his from 1805, and the 1884 editor copied blindly from 1818, despite the warning error ' 1594 ' for ' 1549 ' on the title-page. The last editor (1934), while continuing all but the most obvious errors, corrected ' innorne Leid '.

Copying MSS., and checking texts and proofs, is a laborious task, however, and Monro's latest editor will be fortunate if he has escaped all errors. But at least he believes that they will be his own and not another's.

Note I. CHARTERS OF THE LORDS OF THE ISLES

Of the many charters granted by the Lords of the Isles, it is perhaps not surprising that comparatively few have survived. Some grants of land were apparently never written down at all, but committed to memory by a time-honoured formula, or even carved on a rock on the shore (*Stat. Acc.*, xix 311; *New Stat. Acc.*, vii (Argyle) 384, 635-6). Others, drawn up and sealed in feudal form, were burned, destroyed or lost through war or other causes during the feuds among those who once held their lands from the Lords of the Isles (see *e.g. R.M.S.*, ii 155-56 (712), 638 (2756), 660 (2835); iii 284 (1272), 340 (1536); *Memoirs of Locheill*, intro. 19; Douglas, *Baronage of Scotland*, 507). Others again only survived these perils to disappear in more recent times and less romantic circumstances, like the one cited below which turned up in a Glasgow lawyer's office twenty years ago after being missing for about a century. Only one Gaelic charter is known to exist today.

Those that remain, however, or of which we have sure knowledge, are enough to provide an interesting study. I have seen the originals, copies or authentic references to some forty charters (apart from other deeds) granted by the four successive Lords of the Isles, and in ten of them there is specific mention of their Council. The following are particulars of these ten, with the names of the witnesses where they are on record:—

Inverness, 11 *February* 1443/4. Charter by Alexander Earl of Ross and Lord of the Isles, '*ex matura deliberatione Consilii nostri*', to Malcolm Mackintosh of lands in Lochaber. (MS. 'Macdonald Collections', ii 109-11, in Scottish Record Office, from original *penes* Mackintosh; *Clan Donald*, i 533-4.)

Witnessed by—

Lachlano McGilleon Domino de Dowart
Joanne murchardi McGilleon Domino de Canlochbouye
Joanne Lachlani McGilleon Domino de Colla
Vylando de Cheshelm
Georgio Munro domino de Foulis
Nigello McLoyd

Dingwall, 2 *February* 1462/3. Charter by John Earl of Ross and Lord of the Isles, '*de assensu et consensu et matura deliberatione totius concilii*

sui', to his brother Celestine of the lands of Lochbryne, Lochalsche, &c. (*Reg. Mag. Sig.*, i 783 (806), 21 August 1464.)
[*No witnesses named.*]

Dingwall, 12 April 1463. Charter by John Earl of Ross and Lord of the Isles, '*de consensu et matura deliberatione concilii sui*', to Thomas Dingwall the younger, of the lands of Usuy in Ross. (*Reg. Mag. Sig.*, i 171 (801), 14 August 1464.)

Witnessed by—

Donaldo de Insulis dom. de Dunnowage et de Glynnys
Celestino de Insulis de Lochalch et de Lochbryn
Lachlano McGilleoin dom. de Deward
Joh. de Munro dom. de Foulis tunc temporis ballivo dicti comitis
Lachlano juvene McGilleoin filio et herede dicti Lachlani M. de Deward
Ranaldo Albo de Insulis fratre dict. Donaldi
Joh. Ranaldi Goffridi
Joh. McGeir de Ulva
Eugenio Donaldi senescallo domus dicti comitis
Hectore Torquelli Ingelli [Nigelli ?]
Donaldo McDuffee
Tho. de Munro secretario dicti comitis

Dingwall, 8 November 1463. Charter by John Earl of Ross and Lord of the Isles, '*de assensu et consensu et matura deliberatione totius concilii sui*', to his brother Celestine of the lands of Slete. (*Reg. Mag. Sig.*, i 173-4 (806), 21 August 1464).

Witnessed by—

Joh. de Insulis filio et herede Donaldi de Insulis dom. de Dunnowage et de Glynnis
Lachlanno McGilleone de Dowarde
Joh. Alexandri de Insulis
Joh. Hectoris McGilleone
Angusio Alexandri de Insulis
Eugenio Donaldi Lachlanni

Dingwall, 10 January 1463/4. Charter by John Earl of Ross and Lord of the Isles, '*de consensu assensu et matura deliberacione tocius nostri consilii*', to his brother Celestine of the lands of Fernacostrech. (Original in Scottish Record Office ; *Munro of Foulis Writs*, 7 (21) ; see also *Reg. Mag. Sig.*, i 173 (806), 21 August 1464.)
[*No witnesses.*]

Ayremore, 25 April 1467. Charter by John Earl of Ross and Lord of the Isles, '*de consensu assensu et matura deliberacione tocius nostri consilii*', to his brother Celestine of the lands of Strathalmadale. (*Clan Donald*, i 543-4, quoting 'Macdonald Collections'.)

Witnessed by—

Donaldi de Insulis domino de dunanowaige et de Glynnis
Lachlanno McGilleoin domino de dowarde
Alexandro Johannis domino de Ardnamurchan
Lachlano Juveni McGilleoin Magistro de dowarde

Dingwall, 2 November 1467. Charter by John Earl of Ross and Lord of the Isles, '*una cum matura deliberatione et avisamento totius concilij nostri*', confirming to Abbot Finlay the lands of New Ferne. ('Macfarlan's Note Book', Nat. Lib. MS. 35.4.12[a], from copy *penes* Roderick McLeod of Catboll; MS. 'Macdonald Collections', ii 1309-13; *Clan Donald*, i 541-3.)
[*No witnesses named*: 'This ancient copy goes no further'.]

Dingwall, 6 November 1467. Charter by John Earl of Ross and Lord of the Isles, '*consensu assensu et matura deliberacione consilii nostri*', confirming to William of Cawdor and his wife the lands of Innermerky. (*Book of the Thanes of Cawdor*, 49-50; *Clan Donald*, i 545.)

Witnessed by—

Celestino de Insulis de Lochailch
Lachlanno McGilleoin de Douarde
Lachlanno iuuene McGilleoin senescallo domus nostre
Johanne de Monro de Foulis
Thoma de Dingvale subdecano Rossensi camerario nostro
Lachlanno McFymvyn de Myschenys
Ewgenio Donaldi Lachlanni McGilleoin

Aros, 28 June 14[6]9. Charter by John Earl of Ross and Lord of the Isles, '*de consensu assensu et matura deliberacione tocius nostri Consilii*', to brother Hugh of the lands of Slete. (*Highland Papers*, i 96-9; *Reg. Mag. Sig.*, ii 484-5 (2286), 10 November 1495; for dating, see Beveridge, *North Uist*, 41 note.)

Witnessed by—

Donaldo de Insulis Domino de Dunnowaig et de Glynnis
Celestino de Insulis de Lochalch fratre nostro
Lachlano McGilleoin Domino de Doward
Johanne McGilleoin de Lochboyg
Lachlano juvine McGilleoin Magistro de Doward
Willelmo McLoyd de Glennelg

Rodrico McLeoid de Leoghys
Alexandro Johannis de Ardnamurchan
Johanne Lachlani McGilleoin de Colla
Thoma de Monro nostro secretario ac rectore de Kilmanawik

Oronsay, 1 August 1492. Charter by John Lord of the Isles and Sir Alexander of Lochalsh, '*cum consensu et assensu tocius nostri Consilij*', to John Maclean of Lochbuie of the bailliary of the south half of Tiree. (*Clan Donald*, ii 747-8 and opp. 747; transcript in Scottish Record Office, from original in Lochbuie charter chest; not specifically quoted in Crown charter of confirmation, *Reg. Mag. Sig.* i 465 (2201), 22 March 1493/4.)

With seals of—
Alexandri de Insulis domini de Lochalss
Johannis Abbatis de Y
Johannis Mckayne domini de Ardnamurchoun
Roderici Mcleoid domini de Leowis
Colini Mcneill de Gyrgha

Particulars of the following have also survived:—

14 November 1485. Charter by Angus, Master of the Isles and Lord of Troternish, '*de consensu nostri patris et concilii*', to the Abbot and monks of Iona of the lands of Kilbrenan in Mull. (Register House Charters, no. 517; *Clan Donald*, ii 746-7 and opp. 742).

Witnessed by—
Regnaldo domini insularum filio
Angussio Angussii Mic Regnaill
Lacclanno McMurghaich archipoeta
Hullialmo archiiudice
Colino Fergussii domini cancellario
Terleto Laclani nigri

The presence together of several great chiefs would make the sitting of the Council possible. It should be remembered, however, that witnesses attesting a charter may not always be those present when it was granted (*cf.* Innes, *Legal Antiquities*, 68-69). With this preliminary caution, then, let us set out in the form of an 'attendance record' the names of those magnates mentioned by Monro as having constituted the four groups in the Council. The three charters whose witnesses are unknown have been omitted, and the rebel council of 1545, the chiefs who met the King's Lieutenant at Aros in 1608, and the signatories to the 'Statutes of Iona' in 1609 are added for comparison.

	Inverness Feb. 1444	Dingwall Apr. 1463	Dingwall Nov. 1463	Ayremore Apr. 1467	Dingwall Nov. 1467	Aros ? June 1469	Oronsay Aug. 1492	Ellancarne July 1545	Aros Aug. 1608	Iona July 1609
Maclean of Duart	×	×	×	×	×	×		×	×	×
Maclean of Loch-buie	×		?			×		×		×
Macleod of Harris						×		×	×	×
Macleod of Lewis .						×	×	×		
Mackinnon . .					×			×		×
M^cnaie (?) . .										
Macneil of Gigha .		?					×			
Macneil of Barra .								×		
Clandonald of Kintyre		×	(×)	×		×		(×)	×	×
Macian of Ardna-murchan				×		×	×	×		
Clanranald . .			?					×	×	×
Lochaber Mac-donalds			?					?		
Bishop of the Isles									×	×
Abbot of Iona .							×			

The following witnesses, not included by Monro in his list of members of the Council, can also be identified:—

	Inverness Feb. 1444	Dingwall Apr. 1463	Dingwall Nov. 1463	Ayremore Apr. 1467	Dingwall Nov. 1467	Aros ? June 1469	Oronsay Aug. 1492	Ellancarne July 1545	Aros Aug. 1608	Iona July 1609
Maclean of Ardgour		×	×		×			×		
Maclean of Coll .	×					×		×		×
MacQuarrie of Ulva		×						×		×
Macfie of Colonsay		×								×
Munro of Foulis .	×	×			×					
Chisholm . .	×									

Note J. THE GENEALOGIES

I (Sleat)

Monro is quoted for the descent of Donald Gruamach by Gregory (p. 131), and *mis*quoted by Scott (*Lord of the Isles*, note to first canto, where 'good John of Isla' is called the *last* Lord of the Isles instead of the *best*).

The descent of the family of the Isles has often been the

subject of controversy among historians. In *Clan Donald* (i 526-7), Monro's genealogy of Somerled is given for comparison with those in the Book of Clanranald, MS. of 1450 (or 1467), Books of Ballimote and Leccan, MS. of 1700, and Keating's History of Ireland. Gregory concluded (pp. 9-11), from the uniformity of the Highland and Irish traditions, that the account given by Monro was, on the whole, correct. Skene, when he printed the Gaelic MS. of 1450/67 which he had discovered in the Advocates' Library with a translation (Iona Club, pp. 60, 62), instead of translating the genealogy of the Macdonalds prior to Somerled—which is carried up through the Milesian kings of Ireland to Adam—placed beside it Monro's version of the same genealogy; 'but', he added, 'the reader will bear in mind that the Dean's MS., to which the editor never had access, has been most inaccurately printed'. For comparison, the two are given below:—

1450/67 MS.	*Monro (corrected)*
Somairle	Somerle
mc Gillebrigde	sone of Gillebryde
mc Gilleagamain	McgilleAdam nane
mc Solaime	vic Sella
mc Meargad	vic Mearghaighe
mc Suibne	vic Swyffine
mc Niallgusa	vic Malghwasa
mc Maine	vic Racime
mc Gofrig	vic Gothofreid (Gotheray)
mc Fergusa	sone of Fergus
mc Eirc	McEricke
mc Cartain	vic Carlayne (? Cartayne)
mc Eathach feighlioch	vic Ethoy
mc Collad uais	vic Thola Craisme
mc Eathach doimlein	vic Ethoy dewiff Leist (Ethodius)
	vic Frathriquerwy (fratherus)
mc Cairpre liffechar	vic Clarpre Lisse Chuyr (Corbredus)
mc Cormac Uilfata	vic Chormweil alada (Cormacus)
mc Airt ainfir faulcha	vic Airt Lormeche King of Ireland
mc Cuin cead feaig	vic Chwyn chedchahoy (Condus Centibellus)

II (Isla and Kintyrc)

John Cathanach is described as son of Sir John Mor and grandson of Donald Ballach—leaving no room for an intervening generation—in *Clan Donald* (ii 511, iii 375). The word 'Anald' is unexplained from other sources.

III (Clanranald)

Monro's 'Ean', son of Ragnald and father of Rorey, appears as 'Allan' in *Clan Donald* (iii 227).

Gregory pointed out (p. 30) that John, Lord of the Isles, secured the attachment of the ecclesiastics of the Isles by liberal grants to the Church. Monro's reference to him as 'this good Iohne of Ila' ('ane of the best that came of that sorte'—see No. I p. 144) has caught the fancy of historians and other writers from Sir Walter Scott's day to our own. It is the title of a chapter in *Clan Donald* (i 103-29), and may be found in such books as Anderson (1834), p. 354; James Wilson's *Voyage round the Coast of Scotland and the Isles* (1841), p. 80; Murray (1887), p. 154; Wakehurst (1935), p. 47; Dr Colin M. MacDonald's *History of Argyll* (1950), p. 170; John Mackechnie's *The Clan Maclean* (1954), p. 5; and many others.

Monro does not mention the Glengarry branch (see family tree opposite); but his uncle Hector of Carbisdale is said to have been for some time Captain of Glengarry's castle of Strome on Loch Carron (*Chron. Acc.*, 27), and to have had as his first wife Margaret, daughter of Alexander Macdonald of Glengarry (Mackenzie's *Munros*, p. 350), whose wife was a daughter of the House of Lochalsh (*Clan Donald*, iii 309, 467).

IV (Ardnamurchan)

The pedigree of the Clan Ian of Ardnamurchan, given in the MS. of 1450/67 (and the Book of Leccan), though without a title, is:—'Donald son of Angus son of John the

TREE to illustrate the five branches of the CLANDONALD detailed by DONALD MONRO.
Names and details in red ink are not included in the "Geneologies of the cheiff clans of the Iles".

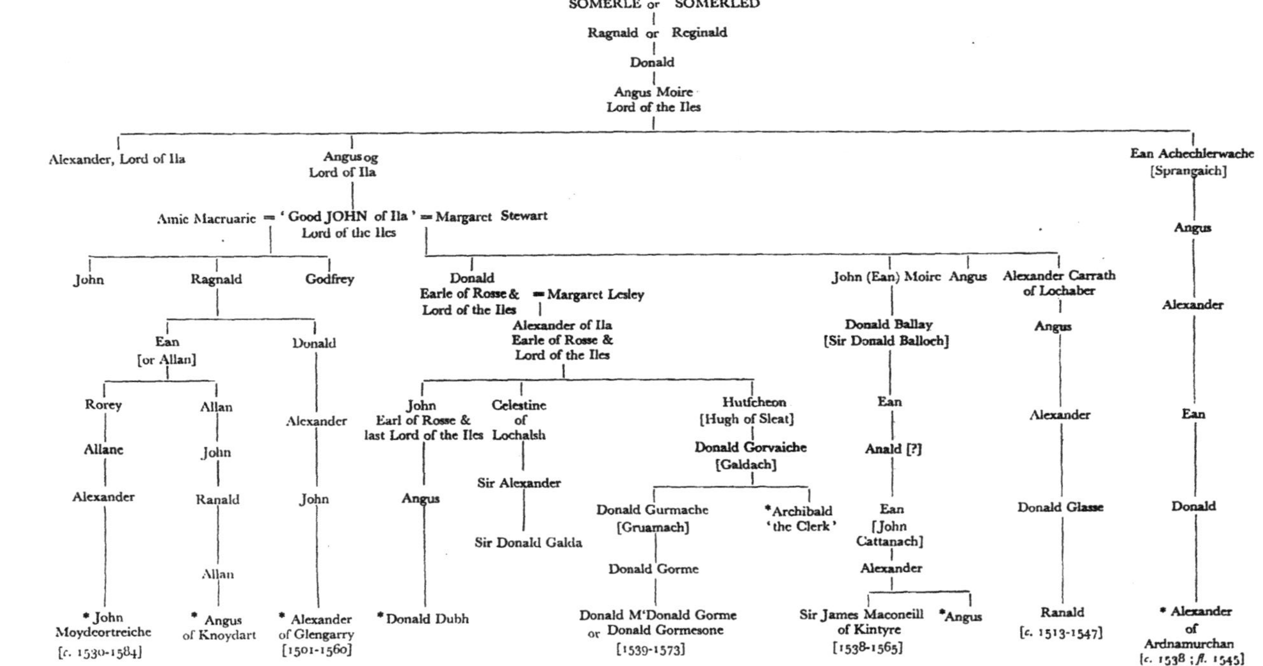

III I II V IV

Dates are those of succession and death.

* Indicates a member of Donald Dubh's "Council of the Isles" in 1545.

bold (sprangaich) son of Angus Mor' (Iona Club, pp. 58, 59, and Skene, iii 469). Monro is among the authorities quoted by Gregory (p. 67) for the Macians of Ardnamurchan. The historians of Clan Donald, who refer to the absence of any reference to the earlier heads of this family in authentic historical records, and the very meagre genealogical details obtainable owing to their disappearance as a territorial house in the first half of the 17th century, say that 'on the early genealogy of the Macdonalds there are no better authorities' than the 1450/67 MS. and Monro's MS. (*Clan Donald*, ii 146, iii 210, and *Scots Peerage*, v 35).

V (Lochaber)

Of Monro's reference to Alastair Carrach as 'the fairest haired man that ever was', the authors of *Clan Donald* (ii 603) say that 'the word *Carrach* has a much less complimentary meaning, and signifies a physical defect, which, in the case of the Lord of Lochaber, may have meant no more than a profusion of warts'.

PRINCIPAL SOURCES

a. The Manuscripts

No copy of Monro's work written by himself is known to exist, although one was ' said to be done from his papers '. The following are details, in the order of their production, of the three later copies preserved in the National Library of Scotland :—

1. The *Balfour MS.* (Nat. Lib. 33.2.3, old no. A.1.12) is in the handwriting of Sir James Balfour of Denmilne and Kinnaird, Lyon King of Arms to Charles I. His name and the date of the transcript appear on the title-page of the thin folio volume—' Ja. Balfourius Kynardiæ/ Miles Leo Armorum Rex/1642 '. Monro's *Description* occupies the first 18 leaves, followed by a transcript in the same hand of the *Descriptio Insularum Orchadiarum* by ' Jo. Ben '. Each of Monro's islands is numbered, making a total of 209, and comparison with Buchanan's *Historia* shows that three considerable groups (totalling 43 islands) have been omitted, either by a defect in the original, or by careless copying. This MS., or one very similar to it, has been published in 1774, 1805, 1818, 1884, 1893 and 1934.

In Balfour's own ' Collection on the severall Shires ' (Nat. Lib. 33.2.27, old no. W.6.15) there is ' A Short Surway of the Vesterne Iyllands of Scotland Lyinge in the Deucalidonian Sea ', which mentions 266 islands. The form of the names is more like Buchanan's Latinisation of Monro than in the above MS., and other resemblances also indicate that Buchanan has here been used.

2. The *Sibbald MS.* (Nat. Lib. 31.2.6, old no. Jac.5th.4.24) is preserved in a bound volume of 31 closely written pages, on the fly-leaf of which is written :—' Ex Libris Bibliothecæ Facultatis Iuridiciæ Edinburgi 1733 '. The handwriting has not been identified, but it has been ascribed to the period between the Restoration and the Revolution, say 1660-90 (Rev. Walter Macleod, in *P.S.A.S.* (1880), xiv 436). The title

has apparently been written over, and the numbers added, in another hand, and marginal notes and interlineations are stated in the Library's (manuscript) Catalogue of MSS. to be by Sir Robert Sibbald, Physician and Geographer for Scotland to Charles II. This MS., which is now published for the first time, lists 251 islands, including the three groups included by Buchanan but omitted from both the other MSS. ; the spelling of place-names is generally nearer to Buchanan's (and sometimes also to those in use today), and most of the alterations are to forms given in the Balfour MS. It has been presumed that this MS. was made under the supervision of Sibbald, who was collecting material for a description of Scotland in 1682-84 ; but in a list of unprinted MSS. given by Sibbald in a work published in 1710 (*Analecta*, i 142) he says of Monro's *Description* : 'the Copie I have (said to be done from his Papers) gives an account of two hundred and ten Isles', which suggests that he did not acquire this fuller version—with its total of 251 islands—until sometime between then and his death in 1722. A copy of it, made under the supervision of the Rev. Walter Macleod in 1879, is in the Library of the Society of Antiquaries of Scotland (MSS. 71), with a note by Sir Arthur Mitchell.

Monro's *Description* fills the first 21¼ pages of the MS. volume, and the remainder consists of another 'Description of the Iles of Scotland', compiled apparently between 1577 and 1582 by an unknown author (who may not have written from personal observation—a statement on Lismore is supported by the remark 'I have honest authors to affirm the same') ; it is quoted in the present volume as the 'Thomas-Skene MS.', as it was known to Captain F. W. L. Thomas, R.N., of the Admiralty Survey, and printed in 1880 in Skene's *Celtic Scotland* (iii preface vii, 428-40).

Sibbald's own 'Description of the isles belonging to the Crowne of Scotlande' is also in the National Library (MS. 33.3.20, old no. A.4.14), and there is a copy in the Society of Antiquaries' library. Following the same order as Monro's, it includes matter from the fuller version of his *Description* and also from the Thomas-Skene MS. (*e.g.* the Eigg massacre of 1577). Sibbald's 'Description' is followed by more detailed accounts of St Kilda and Mull, a very cramped transcript of Monro's *Genealogies* (at p. 66), and Jo. Ben's Latin description of Orkney.

3. The *Macfarlane MS.* (Nat. Lib. 35.3.12, old no. Jac.5th.4.21) is in the third volume (dated 1749) of the 'Geographical Collections' made by Walter Macfarlane of that Ilk, the antiquary and genealogist. It includes both Monro's *Genealogies* (pp. 294-6) and *Description* (pp. 298-347), and, from the omission of the same groups of islands, seems

to derive from Balfour's MS. or the same archetype. Jo. Ben's '*Descriptio*' is placed immediately after Monro, and the whole volume was printed by the Scottish History Society in 1908.

b. Biographical Notices of Monro

Fasti Ecclesiæ Scoticanæ, ed. Hew Scott, D.D., vol. iii, part i [vol. v] (Edinburgh 1870), pp. 299, 302 ; new edition, vol. vii (Edinburgh 1928), pp. 40-1, 45.

'The Rev. Donald Monro, M.A., High Dean of the Isles', by Alexander Ross, Milnton Cottage, Alness, Nov. 1883, in *The Celtic Magazine*, vol. ix (1884), pp. 142-4.

Scotland before 1700, from Contemporary Documents, ed. P. Hume Brown (Edinburgh 1893), pp. 236-8.

History of the Munros of Fowlis, with Genealogies of the Principal Families of the Name, by Alexander Mackenzie (Inverness 1898), pp. 377-9.

Article by Prof. G. Gregory Smith, LL.D., in *Dictionary of National Biography*, ed. Sydney Lee, vol. xiii (London 1909), p. 629.

North Uist, its Archæology and Topography, by Erskine Beveridge, LL.D., (Edinburgh 1911), p. 333 note.

c. Editions of Monro

Description of the Western Isles of Scotland, called Hybrides ; by Mr Donald Monro High Dean of the Isles, who travelled through the most of them in the year 1549. With his Geneologies of the chief Clans of the Isles. Now first published from the Manuscript. To which is added, I. An Account of Hirta and Rona ; by the Lord Register Sir George M'Kenzie of Tarbat, never before published. II. A Description of Saint Kilda, by Mr Alexander Buchan late minister there. III. A Voyage to Saint Kilda in 1697, by M. Martin Gentleman. Edinburgh : Printed by William Auld. M,DCC,LXXIV.

Description of the Western Isles of Scotland, called Hybrides. By Mr Donald Monro, High Dean of the Isles, who travelled through the most of Them in the year 1549. With Geneologies of the Chieff Clans of the Iles, collected by me Sir Donald Monro, Heigh Dean of the Iles. Edinburgh : Printed by J. Stark, for Archd. Constable and Company. 1805.

Miscellanea Scotica. A Collection of Tracts relating to the History, Antiquities, Topography, and Literature of Scotland. (Four vols., Glasgow, I & II (1818), III & IV (1820). Monro's 'Description' at vol. II, pp. 111-53; 'Genealogies' at vol. IV, second part, pp. 121-4).

Description of the Western Isles of Scotland called Hybrides With the Genealogies of the Chief Clans of the Isles By Sir Donald Monro High Dean of the Isles who travelled through most of them in the year 1549. Glasgow: Thomas D. Morison. London: Hamilton, Adams & Co. 1884.

Scotland before 1700, from Contemporary Documents, edited by P. Hume Brown. (Edinburgh 1893.) pp. 238-72.

Geographical Collections relating to Scotland made by Walter Macfarlane. Edited from Macfarlane's Transcript in the Advocates' Library by Sir Arthur Mitchell and James Toshach Clark. (3 vols., Scottish History Society, Edinburgh 1906-8.) (Monro's 'Description' at vol. III, pp. 262-302; 'Genealogies' at Vol. III, pp. 260-2).

A Description of the Western Islands of Scotland Circa 1695 By Martin Martin, Gent. Including A Voyage to St. Kilda by the same author and A Description of the Western Isles of Scotland by Sir Donald Monro. Edited with Introduction by Donald J. Macleod, O.B.E., M.A., D.LITT., Officer d'Academie. Eneas Mackay, Stirling. [1934].

d. Buchanan and his Translators

Rervm Scoticarvm Historia avctore Georgio Buchanano Scoto. Edimbvrgi. Apud Alexandrum Arbuthnetum Typographum Regium. Anno M.D.LXXXII. Cvm Privilegio Regali.

Certayne Matters concerning the Realme of Scotland, composed together: . . . Description of whole Scotland, with all the Iles, & names thereof. . . . As they were Anno Domini, 1597. Imprinted at London for John Flasket, dwelling at the signe of the blacke Beare in Paules Churchyard. 1603. (By John Monipennie. Reprinted in Somers' Collection of Tracts, vol. iii.)

The History of Scotland. Written in Latin, by George Buchanan. Faithfully rendered into English. . . . London: Printed by E. Jones, for A. Churchil, and Sold by S. Crouch, at the Corner of Popes-Head-Alley, over against the Royal-Exchange in Cornhil. 1690.

George Buchanan: Opera Omnia, ad optimorum codicum fidem summo studio recognita et castigata, . . . curante Thoma Ruddimano. (2 vols., Edinburgh 1715.)

The History of Scotland, translated from the Latin of George Buchanan; with Notes, and a continuation to the Union in the Reign of Queen Anne. By James Aikman, Esq. (4 vols., Glasgow 1827.)

e. General

ACCOUNTS: *Accounts of the Lord High Treasurer of Scotland.* Vol. iv, 1507-1513. (1902.)

ACTA DOM. CONC.: *The Acts of the Lords of Council in Civil Causes,* A.D. *MCCCCLXXVIII-MCCCCXCV,* [ed. Thomas Thomson]. (1839.) *Acta Dominorum Concilii—Acts of the Lords of Council in Civil Causes,* Vol. ii, A.D. 1496-1501, ed. George Neilson and Henry Paton. (1918.)

ALLAN MS.: The Tree & Geneologie of the Munro's Barrons & Lairds of Fowlis; in Monro of Allan MSS., H.M. Register House, Edinburgh. (Unpublished, compiled 1734.)

ANALECTA: *Analecta Scotica,* ed. James Maidment, first series. (1834.)

ANCIENT MONTS.: The Royal Commission on the Ancient Monuments of Scotland: *Ninth Report—The Outer Hebrides, Skye and the Small Isles* (Edinburgh 1928); *Twelfth Report—Orkney and Shetland* (3 vols., Edinburgh 1946).

ANDERSON: George and Peter Anderson, *Guide to the Highlands and Islands of Scotland.* (1st edn., London 1834.)

A.P.S.: *The Acts of the Parliaments of Scotland,* vol. ii, 1524-1567 (1814); vol. iv, 1593-1625 (1816); vol. vii, 1661-1669 (1820); vol. xii, suppt. and index (1875).

ATKINSON: Robert Atkinson, *Island Going.* (London 1949.)

BEVERIDGE: Erskine Beveridge, *North Uist.* (Edinburgh 1911.)

BLAEU: *Geographiæ Blavianæ,* volvmen sextvm, qvo liber xii, xiii, Europæ continentvr. (Amsterdam 1662.)

BOSWELL: James Boswell, *Life of Samuel Johnson,* LL.D. (Globe edn., London 1893). *Journal of a Tour to the Hebrides.* (1st edn., 1785.)

BROWN: P. Hume Brown, *Scotland before 1700, from Contemporary Documents.* (Edinburgh 1893.)

BUCHANAN: see p. 151 under *d.*

CALDERWOOD: Rev. David Calderwood, *The History of the Kirk of Scotland,* ed. Rev. Thomas Thomson. Vols. ii and iii (Wodrow Society, Edinburgh 1843).

CAMERON: John Cameron, *Celtic Law* (1937).

CAMPBELL : *The Book of Barra*, ed. John Lorne Campbell. (1936.)

CARMICHAEL : Alexander Carmichael, 'Grazing and Agrestic Customs of the Outer Hebrides', in *Report of H.M. Commission of Inquiry into the condition of the Crofters and Cottars in the Highlands and Islands of Scotland.* (Edinburgh 1884), appendix A, xcix. *Carmina Gadelica* (Edinburgh 1928).

CAWDOR : *The Book of the Thanes of Cawdor, 1236-1742*, ed. Cosmo Innes. (Spalding Club, Edinburgh 1859.)

CHRON. ACC. : *Chronological and Genealogical Account of the Antient and Honourable Family of Fowlis, Chief House of the Numerous and Respectable Name of Munro*, taken from an ancient Manuscript. (Inverness 1805.)

CLAN DONALD : Revs. Angus and Archibald Macdonald, *The Clan Donald.* (3 vols., Inverness 1896, 1900, 1904.)

CRAIGIE : *Dictionary of the Older Scottish Tongue*, ed. Sir William A. Craigie, published to 'Indentit'. (1937- .)

CRAVEN : *Records of the Dioceses of Argyll and the Isles*, coll. and arr. by Rev. J. B. Craven. (Kirkwall 1907.)

CUBBON : William Cubbon, *Island Heritage, dealing with some phases of Manx History.* (Manchester 1952.)

CUMMING : C. F. Gordon Cumming, *In the Hebrides* (new edn., London 1901).

D.N.B. : *Dictionary of National Biography*—see p. 150 under *b*.

DONALDSON : Gordon Donaldson, 'The Scottish Episcopate at the Reformation', in *The English Historical Review*, vol. lx (London 1945), pp. 349-64. See also p. 157 under 'THIRDS'.

DOWDEN : John Dowden, *Medieval Church in Scotland.* (Glasgow 1910.) *Bishops of Scotland.* (Glasgow 1912.)

DYMES : John Dymes, 'Description of Lewis' (1630), in W. C. Mackenzie, *Outer Hebrides*, pp. 591-5.

EXCHEQUER ROLLS : *The Exchequer Rolls of Scotland*, vol. xvi, 1529-1536 ; vol. xvii, 1537-1542 (Edinburgh 1897).

FASTI : See p. 150 under *b*.

FORDUN : *John of Fordun's Chronicle of the Scottish Nation*, ed. W. F. Skene (Historians of Scotland, vol. iv, Edinburgh 1872).

FOULIS WRITS : *Calendar of Writs of Munro of Foulis, 1299-1823*, ed. C. T. McInnes (Scottish Record Society, Edinburgh 1940).

FRASER-MACKINTOSH : Charles Fraser-Mackintosh, *Antiquarian Notes*, first series (Inverness 1865) ; second series (Inverness 1897).

GILLIES : Patrick H. Gillies, *Netherlorn, Argyllshire, and its Neighbourhood.* (London 1909.)

GORDON : Rev. J. F. S. Gordon, *Iona.* (Glasgow 1885.)

GOUGH : Richard Gough, *British Topography.* (2 vols., 1780.)

'GOWRIE': [Wm. Anderson Smith], *Off the Chain*, by 'Gowrie'. (Manchester 1868.)

GRAHAM: Robert C. Graham, *The Carved Stones of Islay*. (Glasgow 1895.)

GREGORY: Donald Gregory, *History of the Highlands and Western Islands of Scotland*. (Edinburgh 1836.) See also under 'Iona Club'.

GRUB: George Grub, *An Ecclesiastical History of Scotland*. (Edinburgh 1861.)

HANNAY: *Acts of the Lords of Council in Public Affairs, 1501-1554*, ed. R. K. Hannay. (Edinburgh 1932.)

HENDERSON: George Henderson, *The Norse Influence on Celtic Scotland*. (Glasgow 1910.)

HIST. MSS.: *Fourth Report of the Royal Commission on Historical Manuscripts*. (London 1874.)

H. P.: *Highland Papers*, ed. J. R. N. Macphail, vol. i. (Scottish History Society, Edinburgh 1914.)

INNES: *Liber Insule Missarum*, ed. Cosmo Innes. (Bannatyne Club, Edinburgh 1847). Cosmo Innes, *Scotland in the Middle Ages*. (Edinburgh 1860.) *Lectures on Scotch Legal Antiquities*. (1872.) See also under 'CAWDOR' and O.P.S.

IONA CLUB: *Collectanea de Rebus Albanicis*, ed. Donald Gregory. (Edinburgh 1839.)

ISLAY: William Macdonald, *Descriptive and Historical Sketches of Islay*. (Glasgow 1850.) [Nigel Macneill], *Guide to Islay*. (Glasgow 1878.) Robert Oliphant, *The Tourist's Guide to Islay*. (Glasgow 1881.) *The Book of Islay*, ed. G. Gregory Smith (1895). Rev. John George MacNeill, *The New Guide to Islay*. (Glasgow 1900.) Islay Archaeological Survey Group, *Archaeological Gazetteer of Islay* (1st edn. 1959, additions for 2nd edn. 1960). See also under 'GRAHAM'.

JAMIESON: John Jamieson, *An Etymological Dictionary of the Scottish Language*. (Rev. edn., 4 vols. & suppt., Paisley 1879-82.)

KEITH: Robert Keith, *An Historical Catalogue of the Scottish Bishops*, ed. M. Russel. (Edinburgh 1824.)

KENNEDY: Rev. John Kennedy, *The Days of the Fathers in Ross-shire*. (New edn., Inverness 1897.)

KINVIG: R. H. Kinvig, *A History of the Isle of Man*. (New edn., Liverpool 1950.)

KNOX: John Knox, *History of the Reformation in Scotland*, ed. W. Croft Dickinson. (2 vols., 1949.)

LESLIE: John Leslie, *Historie of Scotland*, trans. James Dalrymple. (Scottish Text Society, 1888.)

LEWIS: John Lewis, *History of Great Britain*. (London 1729.)

LOGAN : James Logan, *The Scottish Gaël*, vol. i. (1831.) See also under 'McIAN'.

LOWNDES : Wm. Thomas Lowndes, *The Bibliographer's Manual of English Literature* (London 1834) ; new edn., rev. by Henry G. Bohn. (London 1861.)

LYNDSAY : Sir David Lyndsay, *Ane Dialog betwix Experience and ane Courteour*, or *The Monarchie*.

M'ARTHUR : John M'Arthur, *The Antiquities of Arran*. (1861.)

MACBAIN : Alexander MacBain, *Place Names—Highlands and Islands of Scotland*. (1924.)

MACCULLOCH : John MacCulloch, *A Description of the Western Islands of Scotland* (3 vols., London 1819) ; *The Highlands and Western Isles of Scotland*. (4 vols., London 1824.)

MACFARLANE : Walter Macfarlane of that Ilk, *Geographical Collections relating to Scotland* ; vol. ii (Scottish History Society, Edinburgh 1907), vol. iii (ditto 1908).

McIAN : R. R. McIan and James Logan, *The Clans of the Scottish Highlands*. (2 vols., London 1845, 1847.)

MACKAY : David N. Mackay, *Clan Warfare in the Scottish Highlands*. (Paisley 1922.)

—— : John Mackay, *The Church in the Highlands*. (1914.)

MACKENZIE : Alexander Mackenzie, *History of the Macleods* (Inverness 1889) ; *History of the Munros*. (Inverness 1898).

—— : W. C. Mackenzie, *History of the Outer Hebrides* (Paisley 1903) ; *A Short History of the Scottish Highlands and Islands* (Paisley 1906) ; *The Highlands and Isles of Scotland* (1937) ; 'Notes on the Pigmies Isle, at the Butt of Lewis, with Results of the Recent Exploration of the "Pigmies Chapel" there', in *P.S.A.S.*, vol. xxxix (1905), pp. 248-58.

MACKIE : J. D. Mackie, *The Denmilne Manuscripts in the National Library of Scotland* (Historical Association of Scotland, Edinburgh 1928).

MACKINNON : Donald Mackinnon, 'Place Names and Personal Names in Argyll', in *The Scotsman*, 1887-88, esp. 9 Nov., 2 Dec. 1887 ; *A Descriptive Catalogue of Gaelic Manuscripts in Scotland*. (Edinburgh 1912.)

MACLEAN : L. Maclean, *An Historical Account of Iona*. (4th edn., 1841.)

MACLEOD : Rev. Canon R. C. MacLeod, *The Island Clans during Six Centuries*. (Inverness, n.d.)

MACMILLAN : Rev. Archibald Macmillan and Robert Brydall, *Iona : Its History, Antiquities, &c.* (1898.)

MACPHERSON : John Macpherson, *Critical Dissertations on the Origin, Antiquities, Language, Government, Manners, and Religion of the Ancient Caledonians*, &c. (London 1768.)

MAN: [James Man]. *A Censure and Examination of Mr Thomas Ruddiman's philological notes on the works of the great Buchanan.* (Aberdeen 1753.)

MAPS: *The Early Maps of Scotland.* (Royal Scottish Geographical Society, rev. edn., Edinburgh 1936.)

MARTIN: See p. 150 under *c*.

MEGAW: W. Cubbon and B. R. S. Megaw, 'The Western Isles and the Growth of the Manx Parliament', in *Journal of the Manx Museum*, vol. v. (June 1942.)

MILLER: [James W.] *Miller's Royal Tourist Handbook* to the Highlands and Islands. (Oban *c.* 1877.)

MISC. SCOT.: *Miscellanea Scotica*—see p. 150 under *c*.

MITCHELL: Sir Arthur Mitchell, *List of Travels and Tours in Scotland, 1296-1900.* (Edinburgh 1902.)

MONIPENNIE: John Monipennie, *The Abridgement of Summarie of the Scots Chronicles* (1612), reprinted in *Misc. Scot.*, i 175-88. See also p. 151 under *d*.

MUIR: T. S. Muir, *Characteristics of Old Church Architecture &c. in the Mainland and Western Islands of Scotland* (1861); *Ecclesiological Notes on Some of the Islands of Scotland.* (1885.)

MUNCH: *The Chronicle of Man and the Sudreys*, ed. P. A. Munch, rev. Goss. (2 vols., Manx Society, Douglas 1874.)

MURRAY: Mrs Frances Murray, *Summer in the Hebrides—Sketches in Colonsay and Oronsay.* (Glasgow 1887.)

NEALE: [Rev. John Mason Neale], *Ecclesiological Notes on the Isle of Man, Ross, Sutherland, and the Orkneys.* (London 1848.)

NEW STAT. ACC.: *The New Statistical Account of Scotland.* (15 vols., 1834-45.)

NICOLSON: Alexander Nicolson, *History of Skye.* (1930.)

——: William Nicolson, *The Scottish Historical Library.* (London 1702.)

NOBLE: Rev. John Noble, *Religious Life in Ross*, ed. Cameron and Maclean. (1909.)

O.P.S.: *Origines Parochiales Scotiæ*, ed. Cosmo Innes and J. B. Brichan; vol. i (Bannatyne Club, Edinburgh 1851); ii (i) (ditto 1854); ii (ii) (ditto 1855).

PENNANT: Thomas Pennant, *A Tour of Scotland and Voyage to the Hebrides, MDCCLXXII.* (2 parts, London 1790.)

P.S.A.S.: *Proceedings of the Society of Antiquaries of Scotland.*

REEVES: *Life of St Columba*, written by Adamnan, ed. William Reeves, notes rearranged by W. F. Skene (Historians of Scotland, vol. vi, Edinburgh 1874).

REG. OF MIN.: *Register of Ministers, Exhorters and Readers, and of their Stipends*, ed. Alex. Macdonald. (Maitland Club, Edinburgh 1830.)

REL. CELT. : Rev. Dr Alex. Cameron, *Reliquiæ Celticæ*, ed. MacBain and Kennedy, vol. ii. (Inverness 1894.)

RITCHIE : A. and E. Ritchie, *Iona Past and Present*. (Edinburgh 1934.)

R.M.S. : *The Register of the Great Seal of Scotland*, vol. ii, 1424-1513 (Edinburgh 1882) ; vol. iii, 1513-1546 (1883) ; vol. iv, 1546-1580. (1886.)

R.P.S. : *The Register of the Privy Seal of Scotland*, vol. i, 1488-1529 (Edinburgh 1908) ; vol. ii, 1529-1542 (1921) ; vol. iii, 1542-1548 (1936) ; vol. iv, 1548-1556 (1952).

ROBERTSON : William Robertson, *Index . . . of Charters . . . between the years 1309 and 1413*. (Edinburgh 1798.)

ROSS : Alexander Ross—see under *b* p. 150.

ROTULI : *Rotuli Scotiæ in Turri Londonensi* &c. (Record Commission, 2 vols., 1814-19.)

RYMER : Thomas Rymer, *Fœdera Conventiones* &c. (London 1727-35.)

SACHEVERELL : William Sacheverell, *An Account of the Isle of Man . . . with a Voyage to I-Columb-Kill*, ed. Rev. J. G. Cumming (Manx Society, Douglas 1859).

SCOTT : [Sir] Walter Scott, *The Lord of the Isles*. (1815.)

S.H.R. : *Scottish Historical Review*.

SKENE : Wm. Forbes Skene, *Celtic Scotland : A History of Ancient Alban* (3 vols., Edinburgh 1880). See also under ' REEVES '.

SINCLAIR : Rev. A. Maclean Sinclair, *The Clan Gillean*. (Charlottetown, P.E.I., 1899.)

SMITH : J. A. Smith and Rev. Walter Macleod, notes on MSS. in Advocates' (now National) Library, in *P.S.A.S.*, vol. xiv (1880), pp. 436-40.

SPALDING MISC. : *The Miscellany of the Spalding Club*, ed. John Stuart, vol. iv. (Aberdeen 1849.)

SPOT. MISC. : *Spottiswoode Miscellany*, ed. James Maidment, vol. ii. (1845.)

STAT. ACC. : *The Statistical Account of Scotland*, ed. Sir John Sinclair. (21 vols., 1791-98.)

STATE PAPERS : *Calendar of State Papers relating to Scotland*, vol. i, 1509-1589, ed. M. J. Thorpe (London 1858) ; vol. ii, 1563-1569, ed. Joseph Bain (Edinburgh 1900).

STEWART : Malcolm Stewart, *Ronay*. (1933.)

THEINER : Augustinus Theiner, *Vetera Monumenta Hibernorum et Scotorum Historiam Illustrantia*, 1216-1547. (Rome 1864.)

THIRDS : *Accounts of the Collectors of the Thirds of the Benefices, 1561-72*, ed. Gordon Donaldson. (Scottish History Society, Edinburgh 1949.)

THOMAS : Captain F. W. L. Thomas, 'Traditions of the Morrisons (Clan MacGhillemhuire), Hereditary Judges of Lewis', in *P.S.A.S.*, vol. xii (1878), pp. 503-56. See also p. 148 under *a*.

TRENHOLME : Rev. E. C. Trenholme, *The Story of Iona.* (Edinburgh 1909.)

TYTLER : P. Fraser Tytler, *History of Scotland.* (New edn., 4 vols., 1879.)

UNIVERSALL KIRK : *Acts and Proceedings of the General Assemblies of the Kirk of Scotland* [otherwise *The Booke of the Universall Kirk of Scotland*], part first 1560-77. (Maitland Club, Edinburgh 1839.)

WAKEHURST : John de Vere Loder [Viscount Wakehurst], *Colonsay and Oronsay.* (1935.)

WALCOTT : Mackenzie E. C. Walcott, *Scoti-Monasticon : The Ancient Church of Scotland.* (London 1874.)

WATSON : W. J. Watson, *Place Names of Ross and Cromarty* (Inverness 1904) ; *Ross and Cromarty* (Cambridge County Geographies, 1924) ; *The History of the Celtic Place-Names of Scotland* (1926) ; 'Aoibhinn an Obair an t-Sealg', in *Celtic Review*, vol. ix (1913-14).

W.C.P. : *West Coast of Scotland Pilot* (H.M.S.O., London).

WODROW : Rev. Robert Wodrow, *Collections upon the Lives of the Reformers and Most Eminent Ministers of the Church of Scotland* (Maitland Club, Glasgow 1834) ; *The Miscellany of the Wodrow Society*, ed. David Laing, vol. i (Edinburgh 1844).

WORSAAE : J. J. A. Worsaae, *An Account of the Danes and Norwegians in England, Scotland, and Ireland.* (London 1852.)

GLOSSARY

aire : our
armin : steward
awiners : owners

belly flauchts : to bring the skin overhead
bourie : burrow
bourtrie : elder tree
bow (239) : arch (see below)

bruikit : owned
by : forby, also

cheek : side
cleck : hatch
colk : eider duck
conyng : rabbit
cordis (100) : suitable (see below)
cows (14) : (see below)

bow, volt (239) : arch, vault. For *Sib.* 'ane Bow made like ane Volt, . . . throw the quhilk Volt' &c. (lines 5-7), *Bal.* has 'bow . . . woylt . . . woylte', and *Macf.* has 'bore . . . Vylte . . . vylte'. The meaning is plain from Sibbald's own 'Description' (p. 44), which has 'a Bow made lyke a vault', and for the second 'Bow' (line 10) he substitutes the word 'arch'. Monro's passage on the Shiants therefore runs : 'On the east side of this isle there is an arch made like an underground vault (or cave), more than an arrow-shot wide, through which we used to row or sail our boats for fear of the horrible break of the sea on the outward side of the point where that arch is', &c. (This seems to be 'Toll a Roimh' at the north-east end of Garbh Eilean, referred to in MacCulloch, iii 326 ; Lord Teignmouth, *Sketches of the Coasts and Islands of Scotland* (1836), i 169-70 ; James Wilson, *A Voyage round the Coasts of Scotland and the Isles* (1842), i 386-7 ; and see map in Muir (1861), opp. p. 168. Mr Robert Atkinson, author of *Island Going* (1949), writes : 'I should have thought it far more dangerous through the arch than through the wide channel between Eilean Mhuire and Garbh Eilean. However, it may be that at certain states of wind and tide there is a quiet channel through the arch when there is a bad sea off the E. point (Bidean a' Roimh).')

cordis (100) : 'to be suitable' (Craigie, i 683-4). For this word in the phrase 'many great montanes and cordis for hunting' (line 7), Sibbald's own 'Description' (p. 20) substitutes 'forests' ; instead of 'montanes and cordis', *Bal.* has 'Merteines & cunnings', *Macf.* has 'mertines and cunnings'. *Buch.* does not help.

cows (14) : *Bal.* and *Macf.* have 'coillis'. Previous editions (except 1908) give 'coelts' (Hume Brown explains as 'colts'), which cannot be found in MSS. ; 1908 edition has 'Coillis ? [Coeltz]'. Sibbald's own 'Description' (p. 9) says 'thair are many Cowes bred in this isle'. *Buch.* does not help.

dais : does, deer
dotit : endowed
douth, but : without doubt
downwith : downwards
draff : refuse of malt

earthit, eirdit : buried
edderis : adders
ew : yew

fat : cask, barrel, vat
flauchts—see 'belly flauchts'
fleiss : fleece
fog : moss
fowmartis : pole cats
furdis : furnishes
fyrit : fired, fuelled

gavill : gable
geir, geire : gear, goods
girs, girsing : grass, grazing
girth : sanctuary
gudes (196) : cattle, live stock
(249) : manures
gustit : tasted, flavoured

halk : hawk
heavin : haven
hedder, heddir, heder : heather
hesill : hazel
holvis : hollows, holes

impe : engraft

keiling : cod
kipper : spawning salmon
ky : cows

laich : low lying
lave : rest
leid : language

mail : tribute
main, mane, mayne : large, great
mansis : manses, parsonage-houses
manurit : cultivated
martrikis : martins
mask : brew
mekledome : size
meklevine (113) : (see below)
murens (178) : perhaps conger eels (see below)

namely : especially
norne : Norse

meklevine (113) : Not in *Bal.* or *Macf.*, and neither Sibbald's own 'Description' nor Balfour's 'Shires' provides a clue.

murens (178) : *Sib.* has 'murens' twice, but in his own 'Description' (p. 37) he has 'murehens'; it is 'murenis' both times in *Bal.* and *Macf.*, but a misreading or misprint of the first as 'marenis' in previous editions of Monro led Jamieson to misplace the word (iii 232, *s.v.* marenis, murenis) : 'perhaps *lampreys* are meant, Lat. *murena*; although Pennant thinks that this fish was unknown to the ancients. *Zool.*, iii 59. It is more probable, however, that this refers to the *Conger eel*, Muræna conger, Linn.' J. L. Campbell thinks this impossible in such a context : 'Monro would not describe an island as being fertile in fish. What is meant is probably the Gaelic *muran*, bent grass, which grows freely on Fuday and which used to be used for thatching in the islands'. It should be noted, however, that Monro uses the English word 'bent' elsewhere (*e.g.* No. 106), and anyhow it is as curious a form of duty as conger eels.

ovir : ore

pailing : thieving
penniestane cast lang narrest : flat stones placed lengthwise
pintill fisch (179) : (see below)
podlokis (180) : kind of fish (see below)

querrellis : quarries, quarry stones

raid : road, haven
rampis : species of garlic
reistit : dried
ruggaris : depredators

schcald : shallow
scheling : sheltering for sheep
schoole : shovel
selchis : seals
settis : seats
skailzie : slate
spuilzeing : spoiling
stark : strong
store : cattle
streker (13) : (see below)
strype : small rill
stwidis (132) : (see below)
sungaittis : sunwise

taides, toddis : foxes
talloun : tallow

pintill fisch (179) : Hume Brown thought this 'probably the pipe-fish', but J. L. Campbell disagrees : 'The pipe-fish is an insignificant fish of no economic value. Whatever the pintill fish were, they must have been a fish or shellfish of some practical value taken at low tide. They may have been sand-eels, caught by drawing a sickle through the sand at low tide by moonlight, and excellent eating ; or they may have been a shell-fish, perhaps the razorfish or *muirsginn* which is found in the sands round Eriskay and often eaten after cooking '.

podlokis (180) : 'name applied to different kinds of fish in different districts of Scotland' (Hume Brown). J. L. Campbell identifies them as 'pollock or saithe, taken in large numbers around the islands at various stages of their development. The name is given in the Oxford University Dictionary as an obsolete form of pollock. The O.E.D. date for the earliest instance is 1602, but Monro's use of the word puts this back by over 50 years'. Mr Campbell thinks the scaleless salmon (line 36) is 'almost certainly' the grey mullet (*cf.* Martin, 130, 151, 156 ; Miller's *Royal Tourist Handbook to the Highlands and Islands*, 1877 edn., 369 ; Beveridge, 330 ; A. R. Forbes, *Gaelic Names of Beasts, Birds, Fishes, &c.* (1905), 380 ; J. A. Harvie-Brown and T. E. Buckley, *A Vertebrate Fauna of the Outer Hebrides* (1888), 202.)

streker (13) : perhaps intended for 'strekes' = extends, stretches ; apparently 'streitest' in *Bal.* (not very clear), and plainly in *Macf.* ; Hume Brown explains as 'narrowest'.

stwidis (132) : horses, mares. The word appears as 'stuidds' (?) in *Bal.*, and as 'studds' in *Macf.* and all previous editions. *Buch.* says : 'in his præter alia pecora greges equarum'.

termis : possesses
tynchell : circuit (see Note D)

vaik, vayke : weak
vair : spring
virne (165) : worm (see below)

volt (239) : vault (see p. 159 under 'bow')

wandis : fishing-rods
wort : malt liquor before fermentation

zeir : year

virne (165) : probably 'worm' (O.E.D.) ; 'corne' written in another hand above second word of *Sib.* 'quhyte virne' (line 16). *Macf.* has 'confeit corne', but *Bal.* may be 'conseil'.

INDEX

References are to numbers in the text, and not to pages

A. The Islands

Monro's list forms the basis of this index. Where possible, the current rendering—in the *West Coast Pilot*, or failing that the Ordnance Survey one-inch maps—is also given *in italics*, with a cross-reference where necessary. If an identification is shown as doubtful (?), or if none is given, reference should be made to Appendix II (pages 116-20)

B. Other Place-Names

(Modern spellings in brackets)

C. Personal Names

www.ingramcontent.com/pod-product-compliance
Ingram Content Group UK Ltd.
Pitfield, Milton Keynes, MK11 3LW, UK
UKHW020133250726
13967UKWH00002B/621

9 780806 350769